Building the Temple to Hold the Glory:

Judgment Begins at the House of God

David S. Webb

Printed in the United States of America

First Printing: 2026

Eternal Kingdom International Publishing, LLC

LIBRARY OF CONGRESS

LCCN: 2026939385

ISBN- 978-1-968815-13-4 - Paperback

ISBN- 978-1-968815-14-1 - eBook

ISBN- 978-1-968815-15-8 - Hardcover

"The glory of this latter house shall be greater than of the former, saith the LORD of hosts: and in this place will I give peace, saith the LORD of hosts."

— Haggai 2:9 (KJV)

A Note from EKI Publishing:

This book is part of a larger Kingdom reading pathway developed through EKI Books. These works are designed to help readers grow from foundational truths into mature Kingdom life, moving from repentance, identity, and inner restoration into transformation, body life, leadership, and deeper revelation. While each book may be read on its own, together they form a broader discipleship framework.

The EKI Reading Pathway

Foundations
- *Repent: U-Turns Required* - Kirkland M. Rite *(Coming Soon)*
- *Baptized: Why Did I Get Wet* - Kirkland M. Rite
- *Sozo: What Am I Saved From* - Kirkland M. Rite *(Coming Soon)*

Identity
- *Unchained* - Kirkland M. Rite

Discern the Times & Understand His Voice
- *The Language of Dreams (title forthcoming)* - David S. Webb *(Coming Soon)*
- *I Am the Sign* - Kirkland M. Rite *(Coming Soon)*

Restore the Inner Life
- *Soul Made Whole* - David S. Webb *(Coming Soon)*

Grow Into the New Nature
- *The New Nature Series* - Kirkland M. Rite *(Coming Soon)*

Walk in Kingdom Life
- *Walking in the Kingdom* - David S. Webb *(Coming Soon)*
- *Escape the Shame of Babylon* - David S. Webb
- *The Unique Factor* - David S. Webb

Build Within the Body
- *Building the Kingdom Through the Local Church* - David S. Webb
- *Building the Temple to Hold the Glory* - David S. Webb
- *Every Joint Supplieth* - Kirkland M. Rite *(Coming Soon)*

Multiply and Lead
- *Spiritual Fathers (title forthcoming)* - David S. Webb *(Coming Soon)*
- *The Elisha Mandate* - Kirkland M. Rite *(Coming Soon)*

Go Deeper
- *A Gospel of Convicts* - Kirkland M. Rite *(Coming Soon)*
- *The Covenant of Salt* - Kirkland M. Rite *(Coming Soon)*

Foundational and Supplemental Works
- *The Noah Generation* - Kevin Rice
- *Cultivating the New Nature: Growing into the Full Stature of Christ* - Kevin Rice

Companion Resources
- *Values for Living Above and Beyond* - Kevin Rice *(Coming Soon)*
- Workbooks and Study Guides - EKI Publishing Team *(Coming Soon)*

Dedication:

I dedicate this book to the faithful remnant who still tremble at the Word of God, who refuse mixture, and who long to see the house of God restored in purity, order, and glory.

I dedicate it to the builders, the watchmen, the intercessors, the shepherds, and the saints who labor in secret, carry holy burdens, and still believe God can have a house He fully inhabits.

I dedicate it to my family, my ministry friends (Chris J., Ralph T., Jason M., David C., Kirkland R. and others) my mentors (Pastors: David C., Kevin L., Chuck Lawrence) and to those voices who encouraged me to write, speak, and preserve what God has revealed. May this work strengthen those who are called to build according to Heaven's pattern and not man's imagination.

David Webb

Other Works by David Webb:

- _Escape The Shame of Babylon_ EKI Publishing 2025

- _The Unique Factor_ EKI Publishing 2025

- _Building the Kingdom Through the Local Church_ EKI Publishing 2025

Contents

Prelude

The House God Will Fill

Introduction: Before a Temple Is Built, a Question Must Be Answered

Can what you are building carry what God intends to place upon it?

Most structures collapse not because they were attacked, but because they were never designed to carry weight. The tragedy of the modern church is not persecution - it is misalignment. We ask for Glory while reinforcing foundations that cannot support it. We cry for Presence while ignoring pattern. We desire power while rejecting obedience.

God has never poured His Glory on anything He did not first measure, design, and consecrate.

"According to all that I shew thee, after the pattern of the tabernacle, and the pattern of all the instruments thereof, even so shall ye make it." (Exodus 25:9, KJV)

Heaven has a design.

Earth is expected to mirror it.

This book is not about constructing buildings. It is about restoring alignment. The temple God is after is not made of stone, wood, or gold - it is made of people.

Living stones.

Consecrated vessels.

Houses built to host the uncontainable.

"Ye also, as lively stones, are built up a spiritual house, an holy priesthood, to offer up spiritual sacrifices, acceptable to God by Jesus Christ." (1 Peter 2:5, KJV)

If you missed that, you will miss the entire book.

God is not looking for a stage.

God is not looking for a schedule.

God is not looking for a brand.

He is building a house He can fill without withdrawing.

And if the house will not be governed, it will never be trusted with Glory.

Why Glory Requires Government

Glory is not a mood. Glory is not an atmosphere. Glory is weight - and weight exposes what is real.

When glory comes, it does not just bless you. It measures you. It tests your foundations. It reveals whether the structure is aligned with heaven or propped up by man. That is why people who play with God eventually get exposed.

God does not pour glory to entertain crowds. He pours glory to establish government - because glory without government is destruction. Glory without government is fire in the wrong hands. Glory without government is power poured into rebellion.

God will not do it.

So if you want glory, you must understand this first: God fills what He governs. God inhabits what He rules. God remains where His authority is honored.

That is why Scripture does not treat presence as casual. When the tabernacle was built, it was not built according to preference. It was built according to pattern - because pattern is government in design form.

"According to all that I shew thee, after the pattern of the tabernacle, and the pattern of all the instruments thereof, even so shall ye make it." (Exodus 25:9, KJV)

He didn't say, "Be creative." He said, "Be obedient."

And when the work was finished - as commanded - then glory came.

"So Moses finished the work. Then a cloud covered the tent of the congregation, and the glory of the LORD filled the tabernacle." (Exodus 40:33–34, KJV)

Order first.

Glory second.

This is why glory leaves houses that refuse government. People want to blame culture, blame politics, blame "the times." But Scripture says judgment begins in the house, not outside it. If the house is out of order, God does not keep pouring to maintain your illusion of life.

He withdraws.

Quietly.

And the machine keeps running.

But the weight is gone.

So hear this plainly: if your house cannot receive correction, it cannot hold glory. If your house cannot submit to truth, it cannot carry authority. If your house protects disorder, it will be abandoned - because God does not put His glory on a throne He does not occupy.

Glory requires government.

And government starts with a throne.

The River Is Not Random

The River is not emotional. The River is not accidental. The River is not God "showing up" because people got loud enough. The River is legal.

It proceeds from a throne. It carries government. It flows where the King is honored, and it stops where the King is resisted. That is why some houses can sing about "open heaven" for decades and never touch it - because heaven does not open for performance.

Heaven opens for alignment.

Scripture does not hide where the River comes from:

"And he shewed me a pure river of water of life, clear as crystal, proceeding out of the throne of God and of the Lamb." (Revelation 22:1, KJV)

The River is not coming from your gift. It is not coming from your personality. It is not coming from your platform. It is coming from the Throne - and that means it carries authority whether you like it or not.

And where the River flows, it is connected to the Tree of Life. Not as symbolism - as reality. The River and the Tree belong together because life is not a human product. Life is a Kingdom supply.

"In the midst of the street of it, and on either side of the river, was there the tree of life…" (Revelation 22:2, KJV)

That Tree did not begin in Revelation. It began in Genesis.

"And out of the ground made the LORD God to grow… the tree of life also in the midst of the garden, and the tree of knowledge of good and evil." (Genesis 2:9, KJV)

That is the reveal: Scripture is not telling two separate stories. It is showing you one government from beginning to end. The Tree of Life was in the garden. It is in the city. The River is from the Throne. The Throne is the source.

The Knowledge of Good and Evil Was Never Heaven's Qualification

The knowledge of good and evil was not the qualification for heaven. It was the qualification for hell.

Adam and Eve were never meant to carry that knowledge. They were meant to live from the Tree of Life - God-life -

government-life - revelation-life. But the moment they ate from the tree of the knowledge of good and evil, man stepped into the judge's seat. Man began measuring reality by human evaluation instead of divine government.

"And out of the ground made the LORD God to grow every tree that is pleasant to the sight, and good for food; the tree of life also in the midst of the garden, and the tree of knowledge of good and evil." (Genesis 2:9, KJV)

That is why "good" is not a compliment in the Kingdom. It is a trap.

Stop Measuring by "Good"

Any time you hear yourself saying, "They are a good person," or "That's a good church," or "They're good people," or "It's a good group," understand what you are really saying: you are speaking from the tree Adam ate from. You are speaking from a system of judgment that makes you the evaluator. You are using the language of the fall to decide what is spiritual.

And if you think that sounds extreme, that is because your vocabulary has been trained by the wrong tree.

How extreme was Jesus about the word "good"?

"And when he was gone forth into the way, there came one running, and kneeled to him, and asked him, Good Master, what shall I do that I may inherit eternal life? And Jesus said unto him, Why callest thou me good? there is none good but one, that is, God." (Mark 10:17–18, KJV)

Because the knowledge that you are "good" is not what qualifies you for heaven. It is what qualifies you for hell.

We were never meant to know the knowledge of good and evil, only the relationship with a good Father - God.

Hell is full of "good people" who never bowed to government. Hell is full of moral men who stayed self-ruled. Hell is full of religious performers who ate the wrong tree and called it wisdom.

Why? Here is what Jesus said:

"Jesus saith unto him, I am the way, the truth, and the life: no man cometh unto the Father, but by me." (John 14:6, KJV)

There is only one way, and it is not our goodness.

So we need to seriously adjust our vocabulary with this revelation.

Stop chasing "good." Stop defending "good." Stop measuring by "good."

The Kingdom is not built on "good." The Kingdom is built on the Tree of Life - on the River - on the Throne - on the Lamb.

"And he shewed me a pure river of water of life, clear as crystal, proceeding out of the throne of God and of the Lamb." (Revelation 22:1, KJV)

"In the midst of the street of it, and on either side of the river, was there the tree of life…" (Revelation 22:2, KJV)

And if you keep eating from the tree of good and evil, you will stay spiritually blind while calling yourself mature.

And what blocks the River is not "lack of hunger." It is uncleanness. It is disorder. It is spiritual fornication. It is idolatry hiding behind the word "good."

That is why this book will press this until it breaks every excuse: you are not called to be "good." You are called to be spiritual. Because "good" without government is just the knowledge of good and evil - and that tree is not life.

So if you want the River, stop treating it like a random blessing.

It is not random. It is measured. It is governed. It flows where the Throne is honored. And it stops where self is still ruling.

Conclusion: The House Will Be Measured Before It Is Filled

The goal is not to build something impressive. The goal is to build something habitable.

God does not fill what He does not govern. He does not pour glory on what He cannot trust. And He does not release the River into a house that refuses alignment. That is why this book starts with government - because government is not an add-on. Government is the foundation.

If the throne is not settled, everything else is religious activity pretending to be life. If correction is hated, glory will not remain. If order is rejected, the River will be restricted. If uncleanness is protected, heaven will withdraw - quietly - while the machine keeps running.

So understand what you are stepping into: this is not a motivational book. This is a measuring book. It is a pattern book. It is a government book - because the Glory you say you want is weight, and weight exposes what cannot stand.

You are not being invited into a moment.

You are being summoned into alignment.

Order first.

Glory second.

Throne first.

River second.

And if you will let the King govern what you've protected, the house can be built the way heaven intended - from the beginning. Not for display.

For dwelling.

Scripture Index

- Exodus 25:9
- Exodus 40:33–34
- 1 Peter 2:5
- 1 Peter 4:17
- Genesis 2:9
- Mark 10:17–18
- John 14:6
- Revelation 22:1
- Revelation 22:2

Chapter One

Vision Is Government, Not Inspiration

Introduction: God Does Not Build What He Does Not Govern

If you want God's flow, you don't start with feelings. You start with government - because the moment you start asking for the River, heaven points at the Throne. If you want the River, then you have to deal with the Throne. You have to deal with Lordship. You have to deal with God's government in your life.

That is the part people try to skip.

They want "open heaven" language with a closed heart. They want "glory" results with private rebellion. They want kingdom benefits while staying self-governed. And then they act confused when nothing changes.

Vision is not inspiration. Vision is government.

When vision is absent, people don't just "struggle." They collapse into disorder because nothing is ruling them.

"Where there is no vision, the people perish: but he that keepeth the law, happy is he." (Proverbs 29:18, KJV)

This is not poetry. It is a verdict.

And that word "perish" is not soft. It is not just "they have a hard time." It is decay language. It is what happens when something is left ungoverned. It rots. It breaks down. It loses structure from the inside out. People don't "stay the same" without vision - they deteriorate.

That is why this chapter starts cutting: Don't give me this mess that you are a Christian but do whatever you want to do. That is not Christianity. That is a religious veneer - something glued on top of a life that still belongs to you.

You say, "I love the Lord." But you refuse His rule.

No. You don't love the Lord. You love yourself.

That is why Jesus did not teach you to pray, "Take me to heaven." He taught you to pray for government to arrive - Kingdom rule to land in your life until your will is no longer the final authority.

"And he said unto them, When ye pray, say, Our Father which art in heaven, Hallowed be thy name. Thy kingdom come. Thy will be done, as in heaven, so in earth." (Luke 11:2, KJV)

He did not say, "My church go." He said, "My kingdom come."

Because the Kingdom is not a Sunday idea. The Kingdom is the Throne advancing into your life until your will is dethroned and His will becomes law.

So if you want to build a house that can hold glory, stop talking about "presence" while you resist government.

God does not fill what He does not rule. God does not inhabit what He does not govern. God does not endorse what He refuses to own.

That is vision.

And vision always starts at the Throne.

"Perish" Is What Happens Where Government Is Missing

People read *"Where there is no vision, the people perish"* and they hear it like a warning about hardship.

It is worse than hardship.

It is decay.

God has never left man without knowledge. He gave knowledge in His Word. He gave knowledge through His law. He gave knowledge through conscience. And He even gives knowledge in the night when you are asleep - because He is not silent, and He is not unjust.

"For the LORD giveth wisdom: out of his mouth cometh knowledge and understanding." (Proverbs 2:6, KJV)

"For God speaketh once, yea twice, yet man perceiveth it not. In a dream, in a vision of the night… then he openeth the ears of men, and sealeth their instruction." (Job 33:14–16, KJV)

Perish is what happens when something is left without government. It doesn't stay stable. It doesn't remain neutral. It breaks down. It rots. It deteriorates from the inside out. That is what happens to a person, a family, a church, a generation - when there is no governing vision from God.

Because government is built on law. And law is not a human invention. Law is how God holds creation together. There are rules that govern what you can build, what you can carry, and what will collapse under weight - spiritually and naturally. God wired the universe with order, and He wired His Kingdom with order.

"And he is before all things, and by him all things consist." (Colossians 1:17, KJV)

And don't hide behind the excuse, "I didn't know."

God does not judge you for what He never revealed. But He does judge you for what He revealed and you refused. When light is given - through Scripture, through correction, through conviction, even through the warnings He gives in the night - rejection becomes the crime.

"And this is the condemnation, that light is come into the world, and men loved darkness rather than light…" (John 3:19, KJV)

Hosea doesn't let you do that.

"My people are destroyed for lack of knowledge: because thou hast rejected knowledge, I will also reject thee… seeing thou hast forgotten the law of thy God, I will also forget thy children." (Hosea 4:6, KJV)

That verse does not describe ignorance.

It describes rejection.

It says the problem was not that knowledge was unavailable.

The problem was that knowledge was refused.

And the consequence was not mild.

Destroyed.

Rejected.

Forgotten.

That is what perish produces when it reaches full maturity.

So vision is not an option.

Knowledge is not an option.

Government is not an option.

Because when government is absent, people don't simply get "less spiritual." They become vulnerable to anything. They become led by appetite, emotion, culture, fear, and convenience - because something will always rule you. If it is not the King, it will be your flesh.

This is why some people can attend church for years and still decay. The schedule gives them movement, but not government. The music gives them emotion, but not vision. The system gives them routine, but not alignment. And they are perishing in slow motion - rotting while smiling.

Perish does not always look dramatic.

Sometimes it looks normal.

A normal marriage that is quietly dying.

A normal church that is quietly empty.

A normal believer that is quietly compromised.

That is how decay works.

And that is why this book is not gentle about government. Because the house you build without vision will not just "struggle."

It will rot.

Zoe vs. Bios: Two Kinds of "Life"

Most people say "life" and they mean breathing. They mean survival. They mean waking up, going to work, paying bills, staying busy, staying distracted.

That is bios.

Bios is the Greek word from which we derive biological. Bios is your natural existence - your physical survival, your human routine. Bios can be full of motion and still be empty of God. Bios can be busy and still be dead inside.

But the Kingdom is not built on bios.

The Kingdom is built on zoe. Zoe is spiritual life - the kind of life Jesus lived when He walked on earth.

And Scripture does not hide where that word comes from. Revelation calls it what it is: the water of life - and the word used for "life" there is zoe (ζωή). Not bios. Zoe.

"And he shewed me a pure river of water of life, clear as crystal, proceeding out of the throne of God and of the Lamb." (Revelation 22:1, KJV)

In that verse, "life" is **zoe** - God-life - life that proceeds from the Throne.

Zoe is not mere existence. Zoe is God's life - spirit-filled, spirit-led, heaven-governed life. It is the kind of life Jesus would live if He was standing in your shoes. It is not just "living longer." It is living under a different government.

That is why Jesus did not come just to make you "a better person." He came to give you life that comes from God.

"The thief cometh not, but for to steal, and to kill, and to destroy: I am come that they might have life, and that they might have it more abundantly." (John 10:10, KJV)

Bios can be busy and still be dead. Bios can be moral and still be empty. Bios can be religious and still be ungoverned.

Zoe cannot.

Zoe is tied to the Throne. Zoe flows from the River. Zoe is sustained by alignment. Zoe is what happens when God is not just believed in - He is obeyed.

And here is where people get exposed: they want zoe benefits while living bios patterns. They want kingdom flow while staying self-ruled. They want heaven's life without heaven's government.

It doesn't work.

Because the moment you stop living under government, you stop living in zoe. You might still have bios - heart beating, lungs working, schedule full - but you're not living the life the Kingdom calls life.

That is why some churches are full of activity but empty of life. They have bios - human motion, human charisma, human systems - but no zoe. And the proof is always the same: no transformation, no fear of God, no sustained obedience, no weight.

Zoe is not produced by excitement.

Zoe is produced by submission.

So when the Bible says people perish without vision, it is not talking about bios ending. It is talking about zoe disappearing - because when government is missing, the God-life dries up.

That is why the River is called the river of **zoe** - because it is not supplying mere existence. It is supplying heaven's life into a governed vessel.

And what remains is a religious version of survival - busy, loud, familiar, and dying.

God Never Fills What He Does Not Own

God does not rent space inside your life. He does not lease a corner of your schedule. He does not co-sign your independence.

He does not share your throne.

Because the River is not random. It is legal. It has a source, and Scripture names it.

"And he shewed me a pure river of water of life, clear as crystal, proceeding out of the throne of God and of the Lamb." (Revelation 22:1, KJV)

The throne represents God's authority - His government working in your life. The throne is rule. The throne is dominion. The throne is Lordship.

And the River also flows from the Lamb.

The Lamb represents nature - self-sacrifice, meekness, and surrender. The Lamb is how the King rules without compromise. The Lamb is the death of self-will. The Lamb is where you sacrifice sin so God's government can actually rule your life.

If you want "open heaven," you don't start with goosebumps. You start with ownership - because heaven will not pour authority into a life that is still ruled by appetite.

The River carries both: authority and nature. Government and meekness. Rule and sacrifice. That is why you cannot claim you want the Throne while rejecting the Lamb. The same River that brings government also brings a nature - Jesus' nature - into the vessel.

And this is where people lie to themselves. They don't want the River.

They want the feelings of the River.

Like a spoiled kid whining, "I want the river… I want the river…"

No. You don't want the River. You want a spiritual mood that lets you keep your throne.

If you really want the River, you have to deal with the Throne - and you have to deal with the Lamb. Authority and nature. Government and submission. Rule and sacrifice.

If you want government without sacrifice, you don't want the River. You want power without purity. You want authority without the Lamb. And heaven will not pour that.

That combination breaks the fake version of Christianity.

So hear me: don't give me this mess that you are a Christian but do anything you want to do.

That's not "struggling."

That's rebellion wearing church clothes.

Some people have a religious veneer - something laid over the surface to make it appear to be what it is not. A veneer is placed over something weaker or less valuable. It allows the furniture to look better than what it really is. It is a cover designed to impress people while hiding what is underneath. That is what religious appearance does for a life that refuses to be governed.

You say, "Well I love the Lord."

No, you don't love the Lord. You love yourself.

And the proof is simple: you will not surrender what you protect most - your body, your appetites, your secret habits, your right to do whatever you want without consequence.

Scripture doesn't call that freedom.

It calls it ownership conflict.

"What? know ye not that your body is the temple of the Holy Ghost which is in you, which ye have of God, and ye are not your own? For ye are bought with a price: therefore glorify God in your body, and in your spirit, which are God's." (1 Corinthians 6:19–20, KJV)

You are not your own.

So stop praying for heaven to flood a temple you refuse to surrender.

An open heaven means direct access - immediate access - to the Throne and the Lamb. But not every Christian lives like that. Some people may still enter heaven, yet they do not have heaven breaking into earth through their lives - because they refuse to yield the throne.

If your life is out of whack, don't make it mystical. Somewhere there's a throne issue. Somewhere there's a lamb issue.

And until those are dealt with, you can shout "river" all day long and still stay dry where it counts.

Because God does not fill what He does not own.

Vision Without Authority Produces Religious Activity

Vision without authority is not vision.

It is imagination with church language.

Because real vision carries government, real vision carries weight. Real vision tells you what the King has commanded, what the King forbids, and what the King requires. Vision is not "what you want to do for God." Vision is what God is doing - and whether you will submit to it.

That is why people can be "inspired" and still be disobedient. Inspiration does not govern you. Emotion does not govern you. A good conference does not govern you. A strong sermon does not govern you.

Authority governs you.

And hear this plainly: this is not talking about obeying a church leader or their private sin and compromise. Expose it to the light. Don't hide it. The people and church leaders are to follow God and His ways - not look the other way while a leader sins.

Follow the Word.

Follow the Light.

Don't bless the wrong.

Don't hide the night.

"We ought to obey God rather than men." (Acts 5:29, KJV)

And when authority is missing, religion replaces it with activity. Busy replaces obedience. Motion replaces alignment. People start calling movement "growth" because it looks alive, but it is just noise without government.

Man is full of sin - and so are church leaders. Scripture does not flatter the human heart.

"The heart is deceitful above all things, and desperately wicked: who can know it?" (Jeremiah 17:9, KJV)

So if your definition of "submission" is "ignore what's wrong," you are not submitted - you are deceived.

This is why churches can be full and still be weak. They can have programs and still have no power. They can have worship teams and still have no authority. They can have preaching and still have no repentance. Because activity is not proof of authority.

And church leaders are who Jesus corrected the most, because they wanted to be in control, not God.

"Woe unto you, scribes and Pharisees, hypocrites! for ye are like unto whited sepulchres, which indeed appear beautiful outward, but are within full of dead men's bones, and of all uncleanness." (Matthew 23:27, KJV)

Authority produces submission.

And submission produces alignment.

And alignment produces flow.

So when you see a house that lives on activity but resists correction, resists repentance, resists standards, resists holiness - what you are seeing is vision without authority. It is a system that learned how to function without the King.

And systems like that always protect themselves. They will tolerate almost anything except government. They will tolerate sin as long as it stays quiet. They will tolerate compromise as long as it stays hidden. They will tolerate deadness as long as it stays stable.

But they will not tolerate truth that demands obedience - because obedience ends the performance.

So here is the verdict: if vision does not produce obedience, it is not vision. If it does not bring you under government, it is not revelation. It is religious inspiration that leaves you self-ruled.

And self-rule always ends the same way:

Activity increases.

Authority decreases.

And the house becomes loud, familiar, and empty.

Presence Is Not Proof of Approval

People confuse presence with approval.

They think because they felt something, God endorsed everything.

No.

A crowd can feel atmosphere and still be out of order. A person can cry in worship and still refuse repentance. A church can have noise and still have no government. Emotions do not prove alignment.

And Scripture makes that uncomfortable on purpose.

Because if you're not careful, you will use "I felt God" to excuse what God is actually confronting.

The most dangerous deception is when God's patience is mistaken for permission. God will allow people time to repent, but time is not agreement. Mercy is not endorsement. Delay is not approval.

Jesus dealt with this directly: people can prophesy, cast out devils, do "many wonderful works," and still be rejected - because works are not the standard.

Obedience is.

"Not every one that saith unto me, Lord, Lord, shall enter into the kingdom of heaven; but he that doeth the will of my Father which is in heaven. Many will say to me in that day, Lord, Lord, have we not prophesied in thy name? and in thy name have cast out devils? and in thy name done many wonderful works? And then will I profess unto them, I never knew you: depart from me, ye that work iniquity." (Matthew 7:21–23, KJV)

Read that again.

They said "Lord."

They had activity.

They had gifts.

They had results.

And Jesus called them workers of iniquity.

So don't tell me presence proves approval.

Presence can be near you while you are still resisting government.

Because God is faithful even when people are not. He will still speak. He will still convict. He will still warn. He will still draw. But if you keep rejecting Him, His nearness becomes testimony against you, not approval of you.

So here is the line that keeps exposing religious Christianity: stop measuring your life by moments.

Measure it by submission.

If you are not obeying, you are not aligned.

And if you are not aligned, you cannot hold what you keep asking for.

Because God does not fill what He does not govern.

Enthusiasm Cannot Replace Alignment

Enthusiasm is loud.

Alignment is costly.

That's why people prefer enthusiasm - because it feels spiritual without demanding change.

You can shout and still be self-governed.

You can sing and still be rebellious.

You can lift your hands and still refuse obedience.

And you can do all of that while convincing yourself you are "on fire."

Fire is not volume.

Fire is submission.

God is not impressed by noise. God is not moved by hype. God is not persuaded by energy. Heaven does not respond to excitement.

Heaven responds to obedience.

This is why the first sin in Scripture was not "doing too little."

It was refusing government.

Adam and Eve did not fall because they lacked passion. They fell because they rejected command. They chose the knowledge of good and evil over the Tree of Life. They chose self-rule over submission.

And that pattern never changed. People keep replacing obedience with enthusiasm because it lets them feel spiritual without surrendering control.

But God measures hearts, not decibels.

"And Samuel said, Hath the LORD as great delight in burnt offerings and sacrifices, as in obeying the voice of the LORD? Behold, to obey is better than sacrifice…" (1 Samuel 15:22, KJV)

Saul was religious.

Saul was active.

Saul had a "reason."

And God called it rebellion.

So don't tell me "I'm excited" like that settles the matter.

Excitement doesn't establish government.

Alignment does.

And alignment is proven when obedience costs you something - when you obey with no applause, no reward, no comfort, no guarantee - because the King spoke.

That is the difference between a church that hosts God and a church that hosts a show.

Shows run on enthusiasm.

The Kingdom runs on alignment.

So if you want the River, don't bring God your hype.

Bring Him your yes.

Because enthusiasm cannot replace alignment.

When God Withdraws Without Announcement

God does not always leave with thunder.

Sometimes He leaves quietly - while the lights stay on, the schedule stays full, the songs keep playing, and everybody keeps calling it "church." That is what makes it deadly. The collapse is not the first sign.

The withdrawal is.

A house can still look successful and already be abandoned. The room can still feel familiar and already be empty. The traditions can still be intact and the authority already lifted.

Familiarity is the camouflage.

And the scariest part is this: people can keep "shaking themselves" like they always did and not realize God is no longer backing what they are doing.

Scripture doesn't hide that warning. It puts it in a man's life so nobody can pretend it doesn't happen.

"And she said, The Philistines be upon thee, Samson. And he awoke out of his sleep, and said, I will go out as at other times before, and shake myself. And he wist not that the LORD was departed from him." (Judges 16:20, KJV)

He wist not.

He did not know.

He didn't feel it.

He assumed yesterday's authority would cover today's compromise.

And he was wrong.

That is how withdrawal happens. God lifts, and the person keeps functioning. God departs, and the structure keeps operating. God removes weight, and the system keeps performing.

Because performance can continue without presence.

Activity can continue without authority.

Noise can continue without government.

That is why you cannot measure spiritual reality by whether the service "went well." You cannot measure approval by whether people clapped. You cannot measure life by whether the schedule is full.

The question is not: did we function?

The question is: did God govern?

Because when God withdraws, the house may still be busy, but it becomes dry where it matters. Correction disappears. Fear of God fades. Compromise multiplies. And eventually the hidden rot becomes public collapse.

Withdrawal comes before judgment becomes visible.

So do not wait until the building falls to admit God left.

Learn to discern weight.

Learn to discern government.

Because if the King is not ruling it, heaven will not keep filling it.

Conclusion: Vision Is Proven by Obedience

This chapter has been saying the same thing from every angle:

Vision is government.

Not inspiration.

Not emotion.

Not activity.

Government.

Because where there is no governing vision, people perish. They decay. They rot from the inside out. They don't stay stable without government - they deteriorate.

And God has never left man without knowledge. He gave knowledge in His Word. He speaks through His law. He convicts by His Spirit. He warns in the night. When light is given, the issue is no longer ignorance.

It is refusal.

So don't insult God by claiming you "want more" while rejecting what He already said.

Because the River that people beg for is not random - it proceeds from the Throne and the Lamb.

Authority.

And nature.

Government.

And sacrifice.

And when those are resisted, heaven does not keep pouring. God does not fill what He does not own. He does not inhabit what He does not govern. He does not endorse what He refuses to rule.

So here is the final verdict:

If vision does not produce obedience, it is not vision.

If revelation does not produce submission, it is not revelation.

If your Christianity does not bring you under government, it is not Kingdom Christianity.

And if you want to build a house that can hold glory, stop trying to replace alignment with enthusiasm. Stop trying to replace obedience with activity. Stop trying to replace government with emotion.

Because God does not build what He does not govern.

Vision always starts at the Throne.

Scripture Index

- Proverbs 29:18
- Luke 11:2
- Proverbs 2:6
- Job 33:14–16
- Colossians 1:17
- John 3:19
- Hosea 4:6
- Revelation 22:1
- John 10:10
- 1 Corinthians 6:19–20

- Acts 5:29
- Jeremiah 17:9
- Matthew 23:27
- Matthew 7:21–23
- 1 Samuel 15:22
- Judges 16:20

Chapter Two

Why God Abandons Structures He Once Filled

Introduction: God Leaves Before Collapse Is Visible

God does not wait for collapse to prove a house is compromised.

He leaves first.

That is what people don't understand. They think abandonment happens after the scandal, after the split, after the ruin becomes public. But Scripture shows a more terrifying pattern: God withdraws while the structure still looks stable.

The room can still be full. The music can still be loud. The schedule can still be packed. And the weight can already be gone.

Scripture already warned that a house can keep a reputation after it loses life.

"I know thy works, that thou hast a name that thou livest, and art dead." (Revelation 3:1, KJV)

A name can remain. A brand can remain. A crowd can remain. And the house can still be dead.

That is why you cannot measure spiritual reality by activity. A machine can run without God. A system can produce motion without authority. A crowd can produce atmosphere without obedience.

Presence is not proof of approval.

Approval is proven by government.

When God governs, correction is normal. Repentance is real. Holiness is enforced. Truth is honored. And the fear of the Lord is not a phrase - it is a weight that keeps the house clean.

But when God stops governing, something always replaces Him. Control replaces conviction. Performance replaces repentance. Convenience replaces holiness. And people call it "growth" because the numbers stayed up.

God is not impressed.

He is not obligated to remain where His authority is resisted. And that is the warning most churches refuse to hear: you can keep functioning after the King has left you. You can keep "doing ministry" while heaven is no longer endorsing it. You can keep using His name while rejecting His rule.

That is why this chapter is not gentle. Because abandonment is not a mood God falls into.

It is a verdict.

It is the judgment of withdrawal - issued against a house that would not come under government while there was still time.

God leaves before collapse is visible.

God Is Not Obligated to Stay

God is not desperate for association. He is not insecure. He does not cling to structures that resist Him.

If a house will not honor His government, He will not keep lending it His weight just so it can keep its reputation. God is not obligated to stay where truth is negotiated, where correction is resisted, and where sin is protected.

Scripture is clear that God does not strive forever with refusal.

"And the LORD said, My spirit shall not always strive with man…" (Genesis 6:3, KJV)

There is a point where God stops contending with what you insist on keeping.

That is why "We've always done it this way" does not move heaven. History does not control God. Legacy does not control God. Titles do not control God. A building does not control God. And a crowd does not control God.

God stays where He is honored. He remains where His rule is received. But when a house resists the Spirit, it forfeits the flow.

"Ye stiffnecked… ye do always resist the Holy Ghost…" (Acts 7:51, KJV)

Resistance is not neutral. It is rejection of government.

But when leaders turn government into performance, when the fear of the Lord is replaced by optics, heaven does not keep endorsing it.

And hear this clearly: the most dangerous season is when God is still giving mercy while the house is still refusing to change.

People misread mercy as approval. They misread delay as endorsement. They misread patience as permission.

No.

Scripture calls that what it is - despising mercy.

"…despisest thou the riches of his goodness and forbearance and longsuffering; not knowing that the goodness of God leadeth thee to repentance?" (Romans 2:4, KJV)

Mercy is not permission. Mercy is time to repent.

And when that time is squandered, withdrawal is not unfair. Withdrawal is just.

Sometimes judgment is not lightning.

Sometimes judgment is release.

"Wherefore God also gave them up…" (Romans 1:24, KJV)

He stops restraining what you chose, and you learn what your throne produces.

Because God will not keep pouring life into a structure that is determined to stay ungoverned.

So stop treating God like He owes you His presence because you showed up.

He does not.

He is King.

And kings do not inhabit rebellion.

Familiarity Masks Departure

Familiarity is one of the enemy's favorite disguises.

Because familiarity makes you assume God is present just because the room feels normal.

Same songs.

Same voices.

Same routines.

Same seating.

Same language.

And people mistake "familiar" for "anointed."

But familiarity is not proof of life.

A house can be familiar and dead.

A system can be smooth and empty.

A leader can be gifted and abandoned.

That is why Scripture warns about a form that looks right while power is gone.

"Having a form of godliness, but denying the power thereof…" (2 Timothy 3:5, KJV)

That is why Jesus warned that a church can have a name that it lives and still be dead. When the Spirit lifts, the machine can keep running and nobody notices at first - because familiarity keeps the illusion alive.

And this is where the danger intensifies: people build their confidence on how things used to feel. They build their faith on nostalgia. They build their discernment on memory.

But memory cannot govern a present house.

Yesterday's visitation does not guarantee today's approval.

A familiar atmosphere can hide the fact that repentance stopped years ago, correction disappeared years ago, and the fear of God faded long ago. And the most terrifying part is that people will defend it - because familiarity makes them loyal to what God already left.

So if you want to discern reality, stop measuring by comfort.

Stop measuring by routine.

Stop measuring by how "normal" it feels.

Measure by government.

Because where government is absent, familiarity becomes a coffin - beautiful on the outside, dead on the inside.

Tolerated Disorder Forces Withdrawal

God does not abandon a house because it is imperfect.

He abandons a house because it refuses government.

There is a difference between weakness that repents and rebellion that negotiates. There is a difference between a stumble and a system. There is a difference between a person fighting sin and a house protecting it.

God will work with the humble.

He will not endorse the stubborn.

That is why tolerated disorder is never neutral. It is permission. It is agreement. It is leadership deciding what God must "learn to live with." And the moment leaders start managing sin instead of judging it, they are not shepherding the house - they are training it to live without the fear of God.

Tolerated disorder always spreads.

Scripture calls it leaven.

"A little leaven leaveneth the whole lump." (Galatians 5:9, KJV)

It starts as "we don't want conflict."

It becomes "we don't want exposure."

Then it becomes "we don't want correction."

And then the house is no longer being governed by God.

It is being governed by comfort.

And once comfort is the government, the River stops. Not because God is mean.

Because God is holy.

"For the LORD thy God is a consuming fire, even a jealous God." (Deuteronomy 4:24, KJV)

Holiness is not optional.

"Follow peace with all men, and holiness, without which no man shall see the Lord." (Hebrews 12:14, KJV)

This is why Scripture says judgment begins inside the house first, not outside it.

"For the time is come that judgment must begin at the house of God…" (1 Peter 4:17, KJV)

So don't pretend tolerated disorder is harmless. It is a spiritual agreement that invites withdrawal. A holy King will not keep filling a house that protects what He condemns.

This is why Scripture warns about a form that looks right while power is denied. That is not harmless religion. That is a structure learning how to function without God.

And once a house learns how to function without God, it will keep functioning after He withdraws - because it has already been trained to survive without repentance.

So let it be said plainly: if disorder is tolerated, government is resisted. If government is resisted, withdrawal is guaranteed. Not always immediately. Not always dramatically.

But inevitably.

God does not leave because He is weak.

He leaves because He is King.

And kings do not inhabit what dishonors their rule.

Activity Continues After Authority Leaves

When God withdraws, the machine does not stop.

That's what makes this so dangerous.

People think if God leaves, everything will shut down. They expect a sign. They expect a moment. They expect the lights to flicker and the microphones to cut out. But heaven does not owe you a dramatic exit.

A house can keep its schedule after it loses its government. A church can keep its programs after it loses its power. A leader can keep preaching after the weight is gone.

That is why Scripture warns you about a form that remains while power is denied. The structure can still look spiritual while authority has already lifted.

And when authority lifts, something else takes over. Marketing replaces conviction. Control replaces correction. Optics replace holiness. And people applaud it because it still works.

But "working" is not the standard.

The standard is government.

This is why Samson is one of the most terrifying pictures in the Bible. He didn't stop moving because God left. He didn't stop fighting because God left. He didn't stop assuming because God left.

He just kept doing what he always did.

Until he learned the truth the hard way.

"And he awoke out of his sleep, and said, I will go out as at other times before, and shake myself. And he wist not that the LORD was departed from him." (Judges 16:20, KJV)

People don't have to stand up and announce, "You have no authority."

They won't have to.

It will show up where hidden things always surface - at the altar.

When you pray and nothing moves.

When you speak and heaven doesn't back it.

When you lay hands and the bondage stays.

When you command and the atmosphere doesn't shift.

That is exposure.

That is the altar exposing what the platform was able to conceal.

So hear this: you can still have activity and already be abandoned. You can still have noise and already be empty. You can still have gifts and already have no authority.

That is why God's people must stop being impressed by movement. Movement is easy. Government is rare.

Because God does not keep pouring His weight into a structure that refuses to be ruled.

The Difference Between Mercy and Permission

Mercy is not God agreeing with you.

Mercy is God giving you time to repent.

Permission is when God stops contending and lets you have what you chose.

People confuse these constantly. They think because judgment did not fall immediately, God approved it. They think because consequences didn't show up in week one, the decision must have been fine. They mistake silence for agreement.

No.

Silence is often restraint.

Delay is often mercy.

God will warn. He will convict. He will expose. He will send correction. He will even speak in the night and seal instruction - because He is not trying to destroy you. (Job 33:14–16)

He is trying to save you.

But if you keep refusing, mercy doesn't last forever. Scripture says His Spirit will not always strive. (Genesis 6:3) Scripture says people resist the Holy Ghost. (Acts 7:51) Scripture says the goodness of God is meant to lead to repentance. (Romans 2:4) And Scripture also says there comes a point where God gives people over. (Romans 1:24)

That is permission.

That is not endorsement.

That is judgment.

And once God gives permission, the house discovers what self-rule produces. The mask comes off. The leaven spreads. The structure weakens. The rot becomes visible. And what could have been corrected quietly becomes collapse that everyone can see.

So do not wait for collapse to repent.

Repent while mercy is still speaking.

Because mercy is the door.

And permission is the verdict after the door was refused.

Conclusion: Abandonment Is a Verdict, Not a Mood

Abandonment is not God "having a bad day."

It is not God being emotional.

It is not God being unpredictable.

It is a verdict.

God leaves before collapse is visible because withdrawal is mercy's final warning. A house can still have a name that it lives and be dead. (Revelation 3:1) A machine can still run while authority is gone. (2 Timothy 3:5) Familiarity can keep the illusion alive while power is denied.

And God is not obligated to stay.

His Spirit does not strive forever with refusal. (Genesis 6:3) When a house resists the Holy Ghost, it forfeits the flow. (Acts 7:51) Mercy is not permission. Mercy is time to repent. (Romans 2:4) But when that time is despised, God can give people over to what they chose. (Romans 1:24)

That is not endorsement.

That is judgment.

And tolerated disorder is not harmless. A little leaven leaveneth the whole lump. (Galatians 5:9) Holiness is not optional. (Hebrews 12:14) Judgment begins in the house. (1 Peter 4:17) God is a consuming fire, even a jealous God. (Deuteronomy 4:24)

So do not wait for collapse to prove God withdrew.

Learn to discern weight.

Learn to discern government.

Because activity can continue after authority leaves. (Judges 16:20) The platform can hide what the altar exposes. If heaven is not backing what you do when you pray, you don't need rumors and critics to tell you - your fruit already told you.

Repent while mercy is still speaking.

Because once withdrawal becomes verdict, the house will learn - publicly - what it refused to learn privately.

Abandonment is not a mood.

It is a verdict.

Scripture Index

- Revelation 3:1
- Genesis 6:3
- Acts 7:51
- Romans 2:4
- Romans 1:24
- 2 Timothy 3:5
- Galatians 5:9
- Deuteronomy 4:24
- Hebrews 12:14
- 1 Peter 4:17
- Judges 16:20
- Job 33:14–16

Chapter Three

Authority Always Precedes Anointing

Introduction: Function Without Authority Is Rebellion

Most people don't rebel by screaming, "I hate God."

They rebel by functioning without permission. They rebel by moving ahead of government. They rebel by doing "ministry" while refusing to be ruled.

And let me clarify what permission is not: it is not a pastor's personality. It is not a board's vote. It is not your own desire dressed up as "calling." Men can confirm what God has done - but men are not the author of authority.

"And no man taketh this honour unto himself, but he that is called of God…" (Hebrews 5:4, KJV)

Jesus said the same thing in plain language. You don't appoint yourself. You don't choose your own commission. You are chosen, and you are sent.

"Ye have not chosen me, but I have chosen you, and ordained you…" (John 15:16, KJV)

And the Holy Ghost does not merely "approve" your plans. He issues assignments. He calls people to works they did not invent.

"Separate me Barnabas and Saul for the work whereunto I have called them." (Acts 13:2, KJV)

That is why "but I meant well" does not excuse disorder. Saul meant well. He had reasons. He had religious language. And God called it rebellion because he disobeyed. *(1 Samuel 15:22–23)*

So hear this: function without authority is not boldness.

It is presumption.

It is a person stepping into a role God did not assign, speaking with a weight heaven did not place, moving with a permission they do not have. And your will - your flesh - will expose you if you do it without God.

Because the flesh always tries to produce its own "work," its own "calling," its own "ministry," and then it demands God bless it. Scripture doesn't flatter that. It names it.

"Not in the lust of concupiscence…" (1 Thessalonians 4:5, KJV)

And it gives the larger principle:

"For all that is in the world, the lust of the flesh… is not of the Father." (1 John 2:16, KJV)

So when ministry is driven by flesh - by recognition-seeking, platform-hunger, control, pride, appetite - it will look like function, but it will carry no authority. It will be busy, but it will not be governed.

Because the Kingdom is not built on talent. It is built on authority. And authority is not assumed - it is established. When God governs, He assigns. He authorizes. He sends. And when He does not authorize, your sincerity does not make it right.

That is the real problem.

Not that people are "trying."

But that they are trying without rule.

And rule always starts at the Throne. The River proceeds from the Throne and of the Lamb. (Revelation 22:1) Authority and nature. Government and sacrifice. If you will not submit to the Throne, you will never carry true authority. And if you refuse the Lamb - meekness, surrender, the death of self-will - you will always substitute control for government.

This chapter is going to draw a hard line:

God does not endorse unauthorized work.

And heaven does not back what God did not send.

Authority Is Established Before Power Is Released

God does not release power first and then figure out who can be trusted with it.

He establishes authority first.

Because power without authority is chaos. Power without authority is destruction. Power without authority is a weapon in the hands of a rebellious will. And God will not arm what He does not govern.

Authority is heaven's legal order. It is permission. It is assignment. It is jurisdiction. It is the King saying, "This is what you are sent to do, and this is the boundary you are not allowed to cross."

That is why you cannot manufacture authority with charisma. You cannot buy it with popularity. You cannot claim it because you "feel called." You cannot inherit it because you have a title.

Authority is established by God.

And when He establishes it, then power can be released without violating holiness.

This is why Jesus moved with authority before anyone saw miracles. His authority was not a stage effect. It was the government of heaven on display. Scripture says it plainly:

"And they were astonished at his doctrine: for his word was with power." (Luke 4:32, KJV)

And again:

"And they were all amazed, and spake among themselves, saying, What a word is this! for with authority and power he commandeth the unclean spirits, and they come out." (Luke 4:36, KJV)

Authority first.

Then power.

So if you want to see power, stop chasing manifestations and start honoring government. Because God does not pour power on a will He has not conquered. He does not release authority into a vessel that refuses obedience. He does not empower rebellion.

And this is where self-appointed ministry gets exposed. It tries to reproduce results without government. It tries to command without jurisdiction. It tries to function without permission.

And the spiritual realm does not respond to titles.

It responds to authority.

That is why some people can shout in prayer and nothing moves. They have volume but no weight. They have activity but no backing. They have language but no jurisdiction.

Because authority is not assumed.

It is established.

And power follows what heaven has authorized.

Calling Does Not Override Government

A calling is not a license to disobey.

A calling is not permission to skip submission.

A calling does not override government.

People hear "calling" and they think it means freedom - freedom to move when they want, speak when they want, do what they want, build what they want. But in the Kingdom, calling is not freedom from rule.

Calling is assignment under rule.

God calls people into alignment, not into independence. He calls people into order, not into self-direction. And when a person treats calling like a personal right, they reveal the real problem: they want power without government.

Even Jesus, the Son, modeled this. He did not treat His mission like independence. He treated it like submission.

"For I came down from heaven, not to do mine own will, but the will of him that sent me." (John 6:38, KJV)

That is not weakness.

That is government.

So if you claim "calling" but refuse authority, you are not honoring calling.

You are using calling as cover.

And that always ends the same way: disorder spreads, accountability disappears, and people start confusing giftedness with authorization.

This is why the flesh loves "calling language." Calling language can sound spiritual while it hides a rebellious will. It sounds holy while it refuses boundaries. It sounds brave while it resists correction.

But the Kingdom does not run on what you feel.

It runs on what God commands.

So here is the line: if your calling pulls you out from under government, it is not calling.

It is your will wearing Scripture as costume.

Because real calling does not override government.

Real calling submits to it.

Anointing Cannot Protect Disobedience

Anointing is not a shield for rebellion.

Anointing is not a substitute for obedience.

Anointing cannot protect disobedience.

People see gifting and assume God approves everything connected to it. They hear results and assume the foundation is clean. They watch influence and assume authority is intact.

No.

God can use a gift while still confronting a vessel. God can speak truth through a mouth He is still judging.

Because gifting is not the same as government.

And here is the clarification that destroys excuses: gifts and calling are without repentance - anointing is not.

"For the gifts and calling of God are without repentance." (Romans 11:29, KJV)

That means God does not change His mind about what He assigned.

But do not twist that into a lie: that does not mean God will keep empowering your disobedience.

The gift can remain.

The anointing can lift.

The calling can still be real.

And the backing can be gone.

God will let your gift expose you if you refuse repentance.

Because anointing is conditional. It is weight entrusted to obedience. And it can be removed.

Saul is the proof.

"But the Spirit of the LORD departed from Saul…" (1 Samuel 16:14, KJV)

Samson is the proof.

"…And he wist not that the LORD was departed from him." (Judges 16:20, KJV)

And David understood this fear, which is why he prayed what people refuse to pray today:

"Cast me not away from thy presence; and take not thy holy spirit from me." (Psalm 51:11, KJV)

So don't hide behind gifting.

Don't hide behind "God used me."

God using you is not the same as God trusting you.

And the altar exposes that faster than your platform ever will.

If your private life is disobedient, the anointing will not protect you forever. It may cover you for a season while mercy is still striving. (Genesis 6:3) It may allow you time to repent while the goodness of God is still leading you. (Romans 2:4)

But if you refuse, you will be handed over to what you chose. (Romans 1:24)

That is not God "being mean."

That is God being holy.

So hear the line: gifts can remain while anointing is removed. Calling can still be true while authority is withdrawn. And when heaven stops backing what you do, no amount of charisma can replace weight.

Because anointing cannot protect disobedience.

Functioning Without Permission Produces Disorder

Permission is not a feeling.

Permission is not an impulse.

Permission is not "I think God told me."

Permission is government.

It is heaven authorizing you to act within a boundary, for a purpose, under a command.

And permission does not come from a control-freak "mini-minister" - the little gatekeeper group that thinks their insecurity is government. Permission does not come from the "small throne committee" that polices what God never asked them to police.

Permission comes from God.

And if God backs it, the mini-minister needs to be rebuked - not obeyed.

Because men do not get to veto what the Holy Ghost authorized.

"We ought to obey God rather than men." (Acts 5:29, KJV)

So, obey God rather than men - but do not use "God told me" to sanctify independence, presumption, or rebellion against rightful order. Because if what a person is doing does not align with scripture, that is not God's voice, and that person needs to be rebuked. Observe and listen to your senior pastor, not the voices competing with him or trying to replace the senior leader, unless it does not match scripture.

And when something is truly from God, it will not need manipulation to survive. God will sustain what He sends. If it is planted by heaven, it will grow. If it is not, it will become nothing.

Jesus said it plainly:

"Every plant, which my heavenly Father hath not planted, shall be rooted up." (Matthew 15:13, KJV)

And the early church recognized the same principle:

"...if this counsel or this work be of men, it will come to nought: but if it be of God, ye cannot overthrow it..." (Acts 5:38–39, KJV)

And when people function without permission, they don't just make personal mistakes.

They release disorder into the house.

Because unauthorized function trains others to ignore government. It teaches people that zeal is enough. It normalizes presumption. It multiplies voices that were never sent. And the moment multiple unsent voices start moving, confusion becomes the culture.

This is why God judges disorder so seriously. Disorder is not just "messy."

Disorder is rebellion made contagious.

It spreads the moment it is tolerated. (Galatians 5:9) It replaces government with impulse. It replaces submission with opinion. It replaces alignment with independence.

And the Church has been trained to celebrate that. People clap for gifting. They clap for confidence. They clap for "boldness." But boldness without permission is not boldness.

It is presumption.

And presumption always produces the same fruit: division, confusion, competing voices, blurred responsibility, diluted accountability, and eventually a house that cannot hold weight.

Because God will not pour glory into disorder.

He does not fill what He does not govern.

So when you see disorder multiplying, do not pretend it is "growth."

It is the evidence that permission has been ignored.

And ignored permission always produces disorder.

Hardcore Example: Mixture Disciples the Next Generation

A man was asked to take over a youth group.

The youth group was large. It had momentum. It had families that wanted their children trained in the Word. Parents weren't looking for a vibe. They wanted discipleship. They wanted their teens learning Scripture, memorizing Scripture, knowing the books of the Bible, and learning how to read and study the Word of God.

God commanded that kind of training.

"And these words... thou shalt teach them diligently unto thy children..." (Deuteronomy 6:6–7, KJV)

But the man had compromise. He had sin in his past that he would not treat like sin. And he had been marked by the spirit of the age - caught up in cultural identity and trying to carry it into the house like it was neutral.

Scripture doesn't call the spirit of the age neutral.

It calls it a course - an operating spirit shaping how people think and desire.

"Wherein in time past ye walked according to the course of this world, according to the prince of the power of the air..." (Ephesians 2:2, KJV)

And Scripture commands you not to be molded by it.

"And be not conformed to this world: but be ye transformed by the renewing of your mind..." (Romans 12:2, KJV)

Parents could see the compromise. They knew the man was still tied to his past - especially on tattoos. And teens watch more than they listen. So while he would publicly say, "You shouldn't get tattoos," he would fist-bump teenagers later and say, "Nice tattoo."

You cannot warn with your mouth and affirm with your behavior.

That is hypocrisy with a youth-ministry badge.

So the influence spread. Teens started getting tattoos too. Parents found out. Then parents started pulling teens. More teens were pulled. What was once a large youth group steadily became a small group.

Because mixture always reproduces itself.

The house wasn't just losing numbers.

It was losing trust.

And then the man carried a second deception: he taught the teens that the Spirit teaches you everything so they don't need to learn how to study the Word. He treated revelation like it replaces discipline.

Yes, Scripture says the Spirit teaches.

"But the Comforter, which is the Holy Ghost… he shall teach you all things…" (John 14:26, KJV) *"…the anointing… teacheth you of all things…"* (1 John 2:27, KJV)

But the same Bible commands study and shows believers searching Scripture.

"Study to shew thyself approved unto God… rightly dividing the word of truth." (2 Timothy 2:15, KJV) *"…they received the word… and searched the scriptures daily…"* (Acts 17:11, KJV)

So the man wasn't teaching Spirit-led truth.

He was using "Spirit language" to excuse laziness, avoid accountability, and protect compromise.

And when compromise needs protection, it will eventually misuse Scripture. That's what happened. He started trying to weaponize Revelation - misusing talk about the Names on Jesus' thigh (Revelation 19:16) - without telling anyone that Revelation comes with a blessing for reading it and a warning against altering it.

"Blessed is he that readeth… and keep those things which are written therein…" (Revelation 1:3, KJV) *"If any man shall add unto these things… and if any man shall take away…"* (Revelation 22:18–19, KJV)

So he changed meaning to protect appetite.

He changed doctrine to protect compromise.

And that is how the spirit of the age becomes idolatry: you sacrifice money, blood, pain, and health to mark yourself with a cultural identity - then you defend it like it's untouchable.

That is not freedom.

That is an altar of idolatry made with a blood sacrifice.

And God already spoke about markings on the body.

"Ye shall not make any cuttings in your flesh… nor print any marks upon you: I am the LORD." (Leviticus 19:28, KJV)

That command wasn't random religion. It was government. God's laws were designed to protect His people, preserve purity, and keep them living longer - not just spiritually, but practically. His ways still produce life.

"Keep therefore his statutes, and his commandments… that it may go well with thee… and that thou mayest prolong thy days upon the earth…" (Deuteronomy 4:40, KJV)

And this is the verdict: the youth minister did not support the house. He did not support the parents. And unfortunately the leadership would not correct the situation correctly. So mixture was allowed to disciple the next generation.

Because a defiled vessel can still pour.

But what comes out is not clean.

And if you pour contamination into young people, you will not build the future.

You will poison it.

Why God Confronts Unauthorized Work

God confronts unauthorized work because it misrepresents Him.

It speaks in His name without His permission. It uses His language without His backing. It claims His authority while resisting His government. And that is not a small problem.

That is spiritual fraud.

Unauthorized work trains people to trust activity instead of obedience. It trains them to follow personalities instead of the King. It creates confusion in the house because multiple voices begin competing for influence, and the sheep no longer know which voice carries weight.

And when that happens, God does not stay silent.

He confronts it.

Because love confronts what destroys.

And government confronts what resists.

Scripture shows this pattern over and over. God does not treat presumption as "zeal." He treats it as rebellion in motion. That is why He judged Korah when he tried to seize priestly authority. (Numbers 16:1–3, 31–35) That is why He struck Uzziah when he entered the priest's office and took unauthorized ministry. (2 Chronicles 26:16–21) That is why He rejected Saul when Saul moved outside command and tried to function by his own logic. (1 Samuel 13:8–14)

Those are not random stories.

They are warnings.

Because the Kingdom is government.

And government does not tolerate unauthorized work.

So if God is confronting something in a house, don't call it "division." Don't call it "negativity." Don't call it "attacks." Sometimes God is confronting what leaders refused to confront. Sometimes heaven is judging what the house protected. Sometimes the King is removing what men kept excusing.

And the reason is simple:

If authority is not honored, disorder will spread.

If disorder spreads, glory cannot remain.

So God confronts unauthorized work before it becomes a permanent culture.

Because He is protecting the house.

And He is protecting His name.

The Altar Exposes What Platforms Can Hide

Platforms can magnify gifting.

But platforms can also hide emptiness.

A microphone can make people sound anointed when heaven is not backing them. A stage can make people look authoritative when they have no jurisdiction. A crowd can confuse volume with weight.

But the altar is different.

The altar does not care about your brand.

The altar does not care about your title.

The altar does not care about your charisma.

When you pray for people, reality shows up. When you command darkness, authority is tested.

Because at the altar you are not performing.

You are pouring.

You are a vessel.

And what is in the vessel matters.

If I hand you a bottle of water when you are thirsty, you will take it and drink it. But what if I tell you I put pee in it? You won't drink it. And if you have any sense, it won't matter if it's a handful or "just a little."

Now here is the part that exposes people: what if it's one drop?

One drop won't change the color.

One drop won't change the smell.

One drop can hide inside the bottle and nobody would know.

So people would drink it if they did not know.

That is what happens when you pray for people at the altar while carrying sin you are aware of but others are not. You are a defiled vessel. You may still pour, but what comes out is not clean. You're offering "water," but it's contaminated. And you don't just harm yourself.

You contaminate the people you're pouring into.

And heaven already told you what clean water looks like.

It is not your personality. It is not your gift. It is not your reputation.

It is the River that proceeds from God Himself.

"And he shewed me a pure river of water of life, clear as crystal, proceeding out of the throne of God and of the Lamb." (Revelation 22:1, KJV)

If what you are pouring does not match that - pure, clear, throne-sourced, lamb-sourced - then you are not pouring life.

You are pouring mixture.

Scripture says it plainly:

"But in a great house there are not only vessels of gold and of silver, but also of wood and of earth; and some to honour, and some to dishonour." (2 Timothy 2:20, KJV)

A vessel of dishonour is not a trophy.

It's a chamber pot.

It's where waste goes.

And sin makes the vessel a vessel of dishonour. If a man refuses to repent, refuses to cleanse, and still insists on ministering, he is functioning like a chamber pot trying to pour living water.

That is not ministry.

That is defilement.

And the same passage gives the remedy:

"If a man therefore purge himself from these, he shall be a vessel unto honour, sanctified, and meet for the master's use…" (2 Timothy 2:21, KJV)

So if you have sin in your life and think you are pouring out clean water of life while refusing repentance, you are not helping people.

You are contaminating them.

When you speak to people, reality shows up. When you confront bondage, the question is answered: is heaven backing you, or are you just talking?

That is why people don't have to stand up and announce, "You have no authority."

They won't have to.

It will be obvious where it always becomes obvious - at the altar.

When you pray and nothing moves.

When you speak and heaven doesn't back it.

When you lay hands and the bondage stays.

When you command and the atmosphere doesn't shift.

That is exposure.

That is the altar telling you the truth your platform can hide.

And if that exposure happens, don't blame the people. Don't blame "spiritual warfare." Don't blame "the room." Start with the throne issue. Start with the lamb issue. Start with government. Because authority is not a vibe.

Authority is permission.

And the altar reveals whether permission is real.

Conclusion: Authority Is Proven by Submission

Authority is not a title.

Authority is not volume.

Authority is not gifting.

Authority is not what people call you.

Authority is what heaven backs.

And heaven only backs what heaven governs.

That is the line this chapter keeps cutting back to: function without authority is rebellion. Calling does not override government. Anointing cannot protect disobedience. Gifts can remain while anointing is removed. (Romans 11:29; 1 Samuel 16:14; Judges 16:20; Psalm 51:11)

So stop letting "ministry" language cover flesh. Stop letting "calling" language hide presumption. Stop letting results distract you from government. Jesus did not call you to do your will with His name on it. He called you to submit. (John 6:38)

Because permission comes from God - not from your feelings, not from your ambitions, not from the "small throne committee." If heaven planted it, it will grow. If heaven did not plant it, it will be rooted up. (Matthew 15:13) If the work is of men, it will come to nothing. If it is of God, it cannot be overthrown. (Acts 5:38–39)

And the altar will tell the truth whether you want it or not. At the altar, you are a vessel. What is in you will come out of you. If you refuse repentance and keep pouring, you will contaminate the people you touch. The River of life is pure because it proceeds from the Throne and the Lamb. (Revelation 22:1) If your vessel is defiled, what you pour will be mixture. And Scripture warns that in a great house there are vessels of honor and vessels of dishonor. (2 Timothy 2:20–21)

So here is the conclusion:

If you want authority, submit.

If you want power, obey.

If you want the River, yield to the Throne and the Lamb.

Because God will not arm what He does not govern.

And heaven will not back what God did not send.

Scripture Index

- Hebrews 5:4
- John 15:16
- Acts 13:2
- 1 Samuel 15:22–23
- 1 Thessalonians 4:5
- 1 John 2:16
- Revelation 22:1
- Luke 4:32
- Luke 4:36
- John 6:38
- Romans 11:29
- 1 Samuel 16:14
- Judges 16:20
- Psalm 51:11
- Matthew 7:22–23
- Genesis 6:3
- Romans 2:4
- Romans 1:24
- Acts 5:29
- Matthew 15:13
- Acts 5:38–39
- Galatians 5:9
- Deuteronomy 6:6–7
- Ephesians 2:2
- Romans 12:2
- John 14:26
- 1 John 2:27
- 2 Timothy 2:15
- Acts 17:11
- Revelation 19:16
- Revelation 1:3
- Revelation 22:18–19
- Leviticus 19.28
- Deuteronomy 4:40
- Numbers 16:1–3, 31–35
- 2 Chronicles 26:16–21
- 1 Samuel 13:8–14
- 2 Timothy 2:20–21

Chapter Four

The House Is Built by Alignment, Not Attendance

Introduction: The House Is Built by Alignment, Not Attendance

Attendance is not alignment. Showing up is not submission. And proximity to church is not proof of government.

People keep confusing presence with permission - like God is obligated to endorse whatever a crowd normalizes. But the Kingdom does not move by majority vote. The Kingdom moves by rule. If the King is not governing, the house is not being built - no matter how full the room is.

A room can be full and still be ungoverned. A service can be loud and still be disobedient. A system can be smooth and still be empty. Because the house of God is not built by emotion, and it is not built by routine.

It is built by alignment.

Alignment is not a vibe. Alignment is order under authority. And the moment a house stops honoring government, it starts substituting activity for obedience. People call it "growth" because the calendar is packed, but heaven calls it something else: a form without power. (2 Timothy 3:5)

So hear the warning: if the house is not aligned, it will not hold weight. You can decorate it. You can promote it. You can market it. You can fill it with bodies.

But God will not fill it with glory.

Because God will not inhabit what refuses His government.

Alignment Is the First Proof of Government

God does not build a house on attendance. He builds a house on alignment.

Because alignment is submission made visible. Alignment is the evidence that government is present. When people are aligned, it means there is a ruling voice. It means there is order. It means the house is not being driven by personal preference and private agendas.

And the opposite is also true.

When alignment is missing, you don't just get "some problems." You get disorder. You get competing voices. You get blurred responsibility.

You get leaders functioning without permission and calling it ministry. You get people moving from flesh while claiming "God told me." (1 John 2:16) And once flesh is allowed to speak as if it were government, the house loses clarity, and then it loses weight.

Because the Kingdom is not built on preference. It is built on obedience.

That is why Scripture does not treat government as optional. It says vision prevents decay. (Proverbs 29:18) It says holiness is required. (Hebrews 12:14) And it says judgment begins in the house. (1 Peter 4:17)

Alignment is the first proof that a house is under rule. Without alignment, authority cannot remain. Without authority, the River cannot flow. (Revelation 22:1)

So don't tell me a house is "healthy" because it is busy. Tell me whether it is aligned.

Because alignment is where God builds. And misalignment is where God withdraws.

Misalignment Produces Multiple Thrones

Misalignment is not a personality clash.

Misalignment is a government problem.

Because when alignment is missing, it is not "neutral." It means something else is ruling. It means there are multiple thrones operating in the same house - multiple wills, multiple agendas, multiple directions, multiple voices claiming weight.

And that always produces the same fruit: confusion.

Confusion is not just inconvenient.

Confusion is evidence that government has been compromised.

Because in the Kingdom, government creates clarity. When the King is ruling, the house knows what is commanded, what is forbidden, what is required, and what is not permitted. But when the King is resisted, people start doing what is right in their own eyes - each person becoming their own authority.

Scripture already gave that verdict:

"In those days there was no king in Israel: every man did that which was right in his own eyes." (Judges 21:25, KJV)

No king.

No government.

No alignment.

And everybody becomes their own throne.

Mixing Voices Destroys Weight

A house cannot hold glory with mixed voices.

Because mixed voices produce mixed government.

And mixed government produces mixed fruit.

People act like it's "humble" to let everybody speak, let everybody lead, let everybody "flow." But the Kingdom is not a democracy of impulses. The Kingdom is a government. And government requires one ruling standard.

When a house has multiple competing voices, it doesn't just get "diversity."

It gets division.

It gets confusion.

It gets contradiction.

And eventually it loses weight.

Because weight comes from alignment. Weight comes from one sound. Weight comes when heaven can recognize its own order on earth.

That is why the sheep get scattered when voices compete. That is why people stop discerning truth when leadership is blurred. Because confusion does not create safety.

Confusion creates vulnerability.

And here is what usually happens: leaders tolerate mixed voices because they want peace, and they call it "unity." But unity is not everyone getting a microphone.

Unity is everyone coming under government.

So hear the line: mixing voices destroys weight. The River does not flow through a house that refuses order. The River proceeds from the Throne and the Lamb. (Revelation 22:1)

If the throne is divided, the flow will be divided.

And a divided flow will never hold glory.

Unity Is Submission, Not Agreement

Unity is not everyone having the same opinion.

Unity is submission to the same government.

Agreement is easy. People can agree to avoid conflict. People can agree to keep comfort. People can agree to protect reputation. That kind of agreement is not unity - it is a truce between thrones.

Unity is different.

Unity means the house has one ruling standard, and everyone comes under it. It means the King's voice is above every voice. It means no one gets to keep a private agenda while claiming alignment.

That is why Scripture doesn't define unity as "getting along."

It defines unity as ordered submission under God's rule.

"Endeavouring to keep the unity of the Spirit in the bond of peace." (Ephesians 4:3, KJV)

Unity of the Spirit is not unity of convenience. It is unity produced by the Spirit's government - one Spirit, one rule, one sound.

And the moment a person refuses that, the issue is not "they have concerns."

The issue is rebellion.

Because unity is not agreement.

Unity is submission.

God's Order Flows From Headship

God's order is not optional.

It is structural.

It flows from headship.

Because authority is not scattered - it is established. And when authority is established, flow becomes possible. When authority is blurred, flow is interrupted. That is why houses lose weight when headship is resisted.

Scripture is clear that God is not the author of confusion. Confusion is a symptom of disorder, not a personality problem.

"For God is not the author of confusion, but of peace…" (1 Corinthians 14:33, KJV)

So when a house is confused, you don't fix it by adding more voices.

You fix it by restoring government.

Because headship is how God keeps order in the house. Not control. Not tyranny. Government.

And government produces peace - not the peace of silence, but the peace of alignment.

So the question is not whether a house has "structure."

The question is whether the structure is under God.

Because if headship is resisted, the house may still function, but it will not flow.

You Cannot Build With Independent Spirits

Independent spirits love church.

They just hate government.

They love gifting.

They love platform.

They love influence.

They love being "needed."

But they do not love submission.

And that is why independent spirits always fracture houses. They bring their own agenda into a structure they did not build, then they demand the house adjust around them. They call it "leadership." They call it "discernment." They call it "a prophetic edge."

But it's just independence wearing spiritual language.

Independent spirits are dangerous because they are often talented. They can pray. They can speak. They can gather people. They can look productive. But they are not aligned. And when they are not aligned, they do not build.

They erode.

Because you cannot build with people who refuse government.

And the proof is always the same: they will not stay submitted when correction comes. The moment they are confronted, they become offended. The moment standards are enforced, they call it "control." The moment they are told no, they call it "unfair."

But the issue is not the standard.

The issue is their throne.

And when enough independent thrones gather in one house, the house becomes unbuildable. The King will not pour glory into a structure that is full of private governments.

So hear the line:

You cannot build with independent spirits.

Because heaven does not construct what rebellion still rules.

The House Is Revealed by What It Tolerates

A house is not revealed by what it preaches.

A house is revealed by what it tolerates.

Because tolerance is a government decision. Tolerance is leadership declaring, "This will be allowed here." And whatever is allowed becomes normal. Whatever becomes normal becomes culture. And whatever becomes culture becomes the atmosphere the house lives in.

That is why tolerated compromise is never small. A little leaven leaveneth the whole lump. (Galatians 5:9)

It spreads.

Quietly.

Slowly.

Relentlessly.

And leaders often tolerate it because they want peace. But peace without holiness is not peace.

It is a ceasefire with sin.

And Scripture does not leave room for negotiation: judgment begins at the house of God. (1 Peter 4:17) Holiness is required. (Hebrews 12:14) God is a consuming fire, even a jealous God. (Deuteronomy 4:24)

So if a house tolerates disorder, it is not "being gracious."

It is resisting government.

And when government is resisted, weight lifts. Flow dries up. The River stops - not because God is mean, but because God is holy. (Revelation 22:1)

That is why you cannot build a house for glory while tolerating what defiles it.

A house is revealed by what it tolerates.

And the King will judge what the leaders refused to confront.

Alignment Protects the People

Alignment is not "control."

Alignment is protection.

Because when a house is aligned, the people are safe. The sheep know what voice to follow. Standards are clear. Correction is normal. And the atmosphere is not being dictated by the loudest personality in the room.

When alignment is absent, the opposite happens. Confusion rises. Boundaries blur. Accountability weakens.

Independent spirits gain influence. And the sheep become vulnerable to manipulation, mixture, and hidden sin.

That is why God calls leaders to watch, not entertain. To guard, not perform. To govern, not market.

Because a leader who refuses government does not "stay neutral."

He leaves the people exposed.

So don't sell alignment as harshness. Alignment is mercy. Alignment keeps leaven from spreading. Alignment keeps disorder from becoming culture. Alignment keeps the house clean enough to carry weight.

And if someone hates alignment, they are not fighting you.

They are fighting government.

Because alignment protects the people.

Glory Rests Where Government Is Honored

Glory is not a decoration God adds to a house because people asked loudly.

Glory is weight that rests where government is honored.

That is why alignment is not a side issue. Alignment is the first proof of rule. Misalignment produces multiple thrones, and multiple thrones always produce confusion. (Judges 21:25) And confusion is not harmless - it is evidence that government has been compromised. (1 Corinthians 14:33)

A house cannot hold weight with mixed voices. Unity is not agreement. Unity is submission to the same rule. (Ephesians 4:3)

And you cannot build with independent spirits. They love gifting, but they hate government. They love influence, but they resist correction. They don't build.

They erode.

What a house permits will eventually shape its culture, and culture will eventually shape its atmosphere. A little leaven leaveneth the whole lump. (Galatians 5:9) Judgment begins at the house of God. (1 Peter 4:17) Holiness is required. (Hebrews 12:14) God is a consuming fire. (Deuteronomy 4:24)

So hear the verdict: if government is resisted, glory cannot remain. If the throne is divided, flow is divided. And a divided flow will never hold weight.

The River proceeds from the Throne and of the Lamb. (Revelation 22:1)

So if you want glory, stop chasing feelings and start honoring government. Stop celebrating attendance and start building alignment. Stop tolerating disorder and start restoring rule.

Because God does not build what He does not govern.

And glory rests where government is honored.

Conclusion - Glory Rests Where Government Is Honored

A house does not become spiritual because it is active. It becomes spiritual because it is governed.

This has been pressing from the beginning. Attendance is not proof. Activity is not proof. Volume is not proof. Momentum is not proof. The first proof of government is alignment, because alignment reveals whether the King is actually being obeyed or merely being referenced.

This is where many houses deceive themselves. They confuse motion with order. They confuse participation with submission. They confuse the presence of people with the presence of rule. But the Kingdom of God does not operate by crowd energy, emotional atmosphere, or organized religious motion. It operates by government. And where government is resisted, glory does not rest.

That is why misalignment is never a small issue. It is never just a personality problem. It is never just a leadership tension. Misalignment reveals that more than one will is trying to rule the same house. And when multiple wills compete, the result is always disorder. Where there is disorder, clarity leaves. Where clarity leaves, weight leaves. And where weight leaves, people keep performing as though nothing has changed while heaven has already withdrawn.

God does not fill what He does not govern.

That is the verdict. And it must be said plainly, because the Church has learned how to celebrate things heaven has not endorsed. A room can be full and still be out of order. A ministry can be impressive and still be unauthorized. A system can look strong and still be hollow. Because what gives a house strength is not its appearance. It is the throne it is built around.

If Christ is not governing, something else is. If His voice is not ruling, another voice is. If His order is not being honored, another order is being tolerated.

And whatever is tolerated long enough will eventually be called normal.

That is how houses lose their edge. That is how compromise becomes culture. That is how flesh learns to speak in spiritual language while remaining unsubdued. Men begin to act without permission. Leaders begin to function without order. People move from preference, instinct, offense, ambition, and private desire, then cover it with religious vocabulary. But heaven is not deceived by wording. God does not mistake activity for obedience.

Alignment is what makes government visible.

It is visible when people can be corrected. It is visible when order is honored. It is visible when no one is above submission. It is visible when responsibility is clear, voices are rightly placed, and the house moves as one under the authority of the King.

That is where glory rests.

Glory does not rest where rebellion is managed. Glory does not rest where disorder is renamed wisdom. Glory does not rest where mixture is protected. Glory rests where government is honored.

So the question is not whether a house is crowded. The question is not whether people are talented. The question is not whether the system can produce activity.

The question is whether the throne is intact.

Because if the throne is honored, the house can be built. If the throne is honored, authority can remain. If the throne is honored, the River can flow. But if self is still ruling, then no amount of motion can compensate for what government alone can produce.

Alignment is not optional. It is the first proof that the King is welcome.

And where the King is truly honored, glory does not have to be manufactured. It rests.

Scripture Index

- 2 Timothy 3:5
- Proverbs 29:18
- Hebrews 12:14
- 1 Peter 4:17
- Revelation 22:1
- 1 John 2:16
- Judges 21:25
- 1 Corinthians 14:33
- Ephesians 4:3
- Galatians 5:9
- Deuteronomy 4:24

Chapter Five

God Does Not Build on Mixture

Introduction: Mixture Is a Government Problem

God does not build on mixture.

He does not pour clean water into a contaminated vessel and call it "grace."

He does not bless what you refuse to judge.

And He does not build a future on leaders who tolerate compromise while telling everyone they're "growing."

Mixture is not a small problem.

Mixture is a government problem.

Because mixture is what happens when God's standards and the spirit of the age occupy the same space - and nobody wants to confront it. People learn to talk holy while living blended. They learn to quote Scripture while negotiating obedience. They learn to call compromise "wisdom," and then they act shocked when the house loses weight.

That is why Scripture keeps exposing the same pattern: a little leaven spreads. (Galatians 5:9) Judgment begins in the house. (1 Peter 4:17) And holiness is required. (Hebrews 12:14)

So this chapter is not about minor preferences.

This chapter is about government.

Because if you don't deal with mixture, you won't build anything that lasts.

Mixture Always Reproduces Itself

Mixture never stays private.

It multiplies.

Because what leaders tolerate becomes culture. What culture normalizes becomes identity. And what becomes identity starts reproducing itself in the people.

That is why "just one compromise" is never just one compromise.

A little leaven leaveneth the whole lump. (Galatians 5:9)

It spreads quietly until it becomes the atmosphere.

And once it becomes atmosphere, people stop feeling conviction because they are breathing compromise every week. They stop fearing God because they have been trained to call holiness "extreme." They stop discerning because everything is blurred.

Then the house becomes skilled at one thing: appearing alive while slowly rotting.

So hear this: mixture reproduces itself because it teaches people what is acceptable. It teaches them what to copy. It teaches them what to excuse. And it teaches them how to defend it with spiritual language.

Mixture is not a temptation problem.

It is a leadership problem.

Because if government is clear, mixture cannot grow.

But if government is weak, mixture becomes the teacher.

And once mixture becomes the teacher, you are not building disciples.

You are reproducing compromise.

The Spirit of the Age Disguises Itself as Wisdom

The spirit of the age rarely shows up announcing itself.

It shows up sounding reasonable.

It shows up sounding compassionate.

It shows up sounding "balanced."

Because the goal is not just to tempt you.

The goal is to rename compromise so you stop seeing it as compromise.

That is why the spirit of the age disguises itself as wisdom. It teaches people to call disobedience "growth." It teaches them to call holiness "legalism." It teaches them to call conviction "trauma." It teaches them to call repentance "shame." It teaches them to call boundaries "control."

And if you accept the new vocabulary, you will accept the new government.

Because language is government.

Words set limits.

Words set standards.

Words set what is permitted.

That is why Scripture calls it "the course of this world" - a current that carries people if they don't resist it.

"Wherein in time past ye walked according to the course of this world, according to the prince of the power of the air…" (Ephesians 2:2, KJV)

And Scripture commands you not to be shaped by it.

"And be not conformed to this world: but be ye transformed by the renewing of your mind…" (Romans 12:2, KJV)

So when the spirit of the age tells you, "This is wisdom," test it by government. Test it by holiness. Test it by Scripture. Because the spirit of the age will always attempt to blend with the Church until the Church cannot tell the difference between obedience and compromise.

And once the Church can't tell the difference, it can't repent.

Because repentance requires clarity.

And clarity is what the spirit of the age is trying to erase.

When Mixture Enters, Authority Weakens

Mixture does not just corrupt behavior.

It corrupts authority.

Because authority is heaven backing obedience. When obedience is negotiated, backing is reduced. When compromise is tolerated, weight lifts. When mixture becomes normal, the River stops flowing the way it used to - because the River is not random.

It proceeds from the Throne and the Lamb. (Revelation 22:1)

So if the throne is divided - if God's government is blended with the spirit of the age - authority weakens. People can still have activity, but they lose weight. They can still have programs, but they lose power. They can still have gifts, but they lose authority.

And the altar exposes it. You can preach with charisma and still have no authority when you pray for people. You can teach with skill and still have no backing when you confront bondage. Because the spiritual realm does not respond to your opinions.

It responds to authority.

And authority does not survive mixture.

That is why God judges leaven so seriously: it spreads into everything. (Galatians 5:9) It shifts atmosphere. It blurs standards. It weakens government. And then people start doing what is right in their own eyes and calling it "freedom." (Judges 21:25)

Freedom without holiness is not freedom.

It is rebellion with a worship playlist.

So hear this clearly: when mixture enters, authority weakens.

And when authority weakens, the house starts surviving on performance instead of power.

Mixture Produces a Form Without Power

Mixture is how you get churches that look alive but cannot deliver anyone.

They have language.

They have meetings.

They have music.

They have branding.

They have a schedule.

But they have no weight.

Because mixture produces a form of godliness while denying the power of Godliness. (2 Timothy 3:5)

That is not a compliment.

That is a warning.

A form means it looks right on the outside. It has the structure, the vocabulary, the routines, the culture. But the power is denied because government is denied. Holiness is negotiated. Repentance is softened. And the spirit of the age is allowed to remain as long as it behaves in public.

So the house becomes skilled at appearing spiritual while staying blended. And blended Christianity cannot carry authority, because authority requires clarity.

You cannot cast out darkness while you keep darkness tolerated.

You cannot preach repentance while you protect compromise.

You cannot demand holiness while celebrating mixture.

So the form remains.

But the power leaves.

And most people won't notice at first because the machine keeps running. The music still plays. The crowd still claps. The posts still go up.

But heaven is not backing it.

Because mixture always produces a form without power.

God's Standards Are Not "Old Testament Culture"

When people want to keep mixture, they always reach for the same excuse:

"That's Old Testament."

"That's culture."

"That doesn't apply."

But the reason they say that is simple: they want to dismiss God's standards without repenting.

So they pretend holiness was temporary.

No.

Holiness is not a covenant trend.

Holiness is the nature of God.

And God does not change.

"For I am the LORD, I change not…" (Malachi 3:6, KJV)

That is why Scripture says, *"Be ye holy; for I am holy."* (1 Peter 1:16)

God's standards weren't given to ruin people.

They were given to protect people.

They were government.

They were mercy in law form.

And even the practical protections still matter. God's statutes were designed to keep His people from contamination, preserve purity, and keep them living longer - His ways still produce life.

"Keep therefore his statutes, and his commandments… that it may go well with thee… and that thou mayest prolong thy days upon the earth…" (Deuteronomy 4:40, KJV)

So don't hide behind "culture" when God was establishing government.

Don't call it "legalism" when God was preventing defilement.

And don't pretend you're mature because you can explain away holiness.

That is not maturity.

That is mixture with a vocabulary.

God's standards are not "Old Testament culture."

They are the nature of the King.

And compromise is how the devil keeps people bound while the Church applauds itself for being "kind."

That knowledge does not qualify you for heaven.

It qualifies you for self-rule.

And self-rule ends in death.

But to believe Him is to follow Him.

"If ye love me, keep my commandments." (John 14:15, KJV)

"And hereby we do know that we know him, if we keep his commandments." (1 John 2:3, KJV)

"Woe unto them that call evil good, and good evil…" (Isaiah 5:20, KJV)

So no - compromise is not compassion.

Compromise is the doorway to deception.

The Camp Stays Holy or God Turns Away

People love to talk like the laws of God are "ancient" and "obsolete," like holiness was just a primitive phase.

But they don't even believe that in real life.

Try this: go use the bathroom in the street.

Go do it in broad daylight.

You'll find out very quickly that "laws" still exist.

Not because someone is being mean.

Because government exists.

So don't pretend you're too enlightened for restraint. Don't pretend you're too spiritual for boundaries. If you break natural law, consequences show up. If you break civil law, consequences

show up. And if you break God's law, consequences show up -
because God's government is real.

And here is the part people hate: even if nobody sees it, it
still contaminates the house.

God told Israel that even human waste had to be handled
with holiness because He walked in the camp. That is why they
had to take their waste outside the camp and cover it - so the
camp would remain clean, disease would not spread, and God
would not be walking in that mess.

God does not want to look at your mess.

No more than you would.

Scripture says it plainly:

*"Thou shalt have a place also without the camp, whither thou shalt go
forth abroad… and… when thou wilt ease thyself abroad, thou shalt dig
therewith, and shalt turn back and cover that which cometh from thee: for the
LORD thy God walketh in the midst of thy camp… therefore shall thy camp
be holy: that he see no unclean thing in thee, and turn away from thee."*
(Deuteronomy 23:12–14, KJV)

Read that again: turn away from thee.

God does not negotiate with "unclean."

He doesn't "coexist" with defilement.

He turns away.

So don't tell me God's standards were "Old Testament
culture" when God Himself tied holiness to His presence in the
camp. His ways were designed to preserve life, keep the house

clean, and keep disease and defilement from spreading among the people.

And His nature has not changed.

Compromise Is Not Compassion

Compassion calls people out of bondage.

Compromise leaves them in it and calls it "love."

That is why the spirit of the age always tries to redefine compassion. It teaches the Church to feel sorry for people without requiring repentance. It teaches leaders to protect sin because "they've been through a lot." It teaches houses to lower standards so nobody feels uncomfortable.

But the Kingdom is not built on comfort.

It is built on truth.

And truth confronts.

If you remove confrontation, you remove repentance. If you remove repentance, you remove cleansing. And if you remove cleansing, you cannot carry weight.

That is not harshness.

That is reality.

Because a holy God does not build a holy house by celebrating unholiness.

So when someone says, "You need more compassion," ask them what they mean. If they mean "stop calling sin sin," that's not compassion.

That's compromise.

Then people start thinking they are "good people." The church starts thinking it is "doing good." And without realizing it, they are using the very knowledge Adam ate from - the knowledge of good and evil (Genesis 2:9) - as their measuring stick.

That knowledge does not qualify you for heaven.

It qualifies you for self-rule.

And self-rule ends in death.

So repentance disappears. Faith becomes vocabulary. And "believing in Christ" gets reduced to agreement instead of obedience.

But to believe Him is to follow Him.

"If ye love me, keep my commandments." (John 14:15, KJV)

"And hereby we do know that we know him, if we keep his commandments." (1 John 2:3, KJV)

And once compromise is renamed compassion, the spirit of the age does what it always does: it starts calling evil good and good evil.

"Woe unto them that call evil good, and good evil…" (Isaiah 5:20, KJV)

So no - compromise is not compassion.

Compromise is the doorway to deception.

Mixture Makes Repentance Rare

Mixture does not merely change behavior. It retrains the conscience. Once compromise is normalized, repentance starts feeling extreme, holiness starts sounding radical, and conviction gets mislabeled as condemnation. And the spirit of the age smiles because the Church has been trained to reject the very thing that cleanses it. That is how mixture protects itself: it does not just excuse sin. It conditions the house to resist the very cleansing that could free it.

Repentance requires clarity. You cannot repent of what you refuse to call sin. You cannot turn from what you keep renaming. You cannot be delivered from what you keep defending.

That is why mixture makes repentance rare. It clouds the line. It blurs the boundary. It turns obedience into a discussion and makes holiness negotiable.

And when repentance becomes rare, authority becomes rare.

Because the Kingdom is government.

And government only remains where repentance is normal.

So if you want to know whether mixture is in a house, don't start by measuring how loud worship is.

Measure how common repentance is.

Measure how quickly people obey.

Measure how often sin is confessed, judged, and forsaken.

Because where mixture reigns, repentance becomes rare.

And where repentance is rare, weight cannot remain.

Conclusion: Clean Vessels Carry Clean Water

Mixture is not harmless.

Mixture is government being resisted.

And when government is resisted, authority weakens. When authority weakens, the house survives on form instead of power. (2 Timothy 3:5)

That is why mixture survives so long: it learns to speak in language that sounds wise while resisting the government of God. It renames compromise so repentance feels "extreme." (Ephesians 2:2; Romans 12:2) It teaches people to call evil good and good evil. (Isaiah 5:20) And then the Church starts congratulating itself for being "good," using the language of the wrong tree. (Genesis 2:9)

But the River of life is not mixture.

It is pure.

It proceeds from the throne of God and of the Lamb. (Revelation 22:1)

So if you want to carry life, you cannot pour from a defiled vessel. If you want to disciple a generation, you cannot normalize compromise and call it compassion. If you want the house to hold weight, you cannot tolerate leaven and pretend it won't spread. (Galatians 5:9)

Holiness is not optional. (Hebrews 12:14) Judgment begins in the house. (1 Peter 4:17) God does not change. (Malachi 3:6)

So here is the conclusion:

Clean vessels carry clean water.

If the vessel is mixed, what it pours will be mixed.

And a mixed house will never hold glory.

Because God does not build on mixture.

Scripture Index

Chapter Six

Shame Governs Before Sin Is Visible

Introduction: Shame Is Hell's Favorite Control System

Most people think sin is what controls them.

But shame is what governs them first.

Because shame doesn't just accuse you after you fall - it builds a prison before you ever repent. It teaches you to hide, to manage appearances, to protect reputation, and to avoid the one thing that would actually set you free: truth.

Shame is hell's favorite control system because it doesn't need chains.

It uses silence.

It uses secrecy.

It uses fear of exposure.

And it convinces people that being seen is more dangerous than being bound.

That is why the first reaction after the fall was not worship.

It was hiding.

"And the eyes of them both were opened, and they knew that they were naked; and they sewed fig leaves together, and made themselves aprons." (Genesis 3:7, KJV)

That is not a cute Bible story.

That is the blueprint of shame.

Sin happened - then shame immediately started governing the response. They didn't run to God. They ran to cover. They didn't confess. They constructed.

And here is the part people miss: fig leaves are not repentance.

Fig leaves are image management.

Fig leaves are spiritual cosmetics - something that makes you look "covered" while you stay unchanged. And once shame teaches you to sew fig leaves, you will keep sewing them for the rest of your life unless God breaks the pattern.

Shame does not lead you to repentance.

Shame leads you to hiding.

Shame leads you to silence.

Shame leads you to counterfeit covering.

And then it leads you to a life where you can sit in church, lift your hands, quote Scripture, and still live governed by fear.

That is why Paul didn't treat shame like a minor emotion. He tied spiritual maturity to being able to handle the Word without being ashamed.

"Study to shew thyself approved unto God, a workman that needeth not to be ashamed, rightly dividing the word of truth." (2 Timothy 2:15, KJV)

Read that line again: needeth not to be ashamed.

Shame doesn't just make you sad.

Shame makes you crooked.

Because when shame governs, you don't "rightly divide" truth - you twist truth to protect your hiding. You avoid verses that confront you. You weaponize verses that excuse you. You redefine compassion to keep sin safe. And all the while, shame sits on the throne of your inner life telling you, "Don't let anyone see the real you."

And shame doesn't just corrupt individuals.

It corrupts houses.

Because a shame-governed house will protect appearances over purity. It will reward loyalty over obedience. It will silence correction to avoid discomfort. It will label exposure "division." It will call confrontation "attacks." And it will keep people trapped in the same cycles while pretending everybody is "fine."

But God does not build a holy house on hidden mess.

God does not walk through what you refuse to clean.

And Scripture is blunt about that.

God told Israel that even hidden uncleanness - even things people didn't want discussed - still mattered because He walked in the camp.

"For the LORD thy God walketh in the midst of thy camp… therefore shall thy camp be holy: that he see no unclean thing in thee, and turn away from thee." (Deuteronomy 23:14, KJV)

Shame wants you to believe, "If nobody sees it, it doesn't matter."

God says the opposite: if I see it, it matters.

And shame's entire strategy is to keep you locked in a place where you are more terrified of being exposed than you are of being unclean. That is why shame governs before sin is visible - because it trains you to protect darkness.

So this chapter is going to put a knife right on the root:

Shame is not protection.

Shame is not humility.

Shame is not "wisdom."

Shame is hell's system to keep people bound while they keep smiling.

And it breaks the moment authority is restored - because shame cannot rule where truth is honored, where repentance is normal, and where the fear of the Lord is greater than the fear of man.

Shame Builds Fig-Leaf Religion

Shame doesn't just make you hide.

Shame teaches you to manufacture a cover.

It teaches you to build a religious costume that looks like holiness from a distance but collapses the moment God speaks.

That is fig-leaf religion.

Adam and Eve didn't repent first.

They covered first.

"They sewed fig leaves together, and made themselves aprons." (Genesis 3:7, KJV)

That was the first counterfeit solution to sin: self-made covering.

And it still operates the same way today. People don't run to Christ for cleansing. They run to performance for camouflage. They don't pursue truth. They pursue image. They don't confess. They construct.

They sew.

They manage.

They curate.

They learn how to look "fine."

And shame loves church environments that reward fig leaves. It loves houses where everyone is polished but nobody is clean. It loves systems where people can sing loudly while staying bound quietly.

Because fig leaves are not repentance.

Fig leaves are concealment.

They are what you do when you want the appearance of covering without the cost of surrender.

That is why shame builds religion that is obsessed with being seen as righteous instead of actually being righteous. It produces people who know how to talk kingdom language but refuse kingdom government. They want grace as cover, not grace as transformation.

But Scripture already warned that this exists: a form of godliness while denying the power.

"Having a form of godliness, but denying the power thereof…" (2 Timothy 3:5, KJV)

Form is fig leaves.

Power is transformation.

And shame will always choose form over power because form hides you.

Power exposes you.

So hear the line: shame builds fig-leaf religion because it would rather keep you respectable than set you free.

And that is why some people can sit in church for decades and never repent. They don't need deliverance. They need truth.

Because fig leaves can cover you from people.

But they cannot cover you from God.

Shame Turns Conviction Into Condemnation

Shame has one main goal: to make the voice of God feel hostile.

Because if shame can convince you that conviction is condemnation, you will stop responding to God. You will start running from Him while still using His name.

Conviction is God pointing to sin so you can be cleansed.

Condemnation is the devil pointing to you so you stay bound.

Shame blurs that line on purpose.

It takes the moment God calls you to repent and it whispers, "See, you're trash. You'll never change. You're not real. God is done with you." And if you listen, you don't repent.

You hide.

You shut down.

You sew more fig leaves.

That is why shame is not "humility." Shame is pride in reverse - still self-centered, still obsessed with self, still refusing truth because truth feels like exposure.

And Scripture draws a hard line here. There is a difference between condemnation and the Spirit's work of correction.

"There is therefore now no condemnation to them which are in Christ Jesus..." (Romans 8:1, KJV)

That means condemnation is not your portion in Christ.

But that does not mean you never get corrected. Correction is love. Correction is government. Correction is God refusing to let you stay crooked.

"For whom the Lord loveth he chasteneth..." (Hebrews 12:6, KJV)

So here is the trap: shame makes you interpret chastening as rejection. It makes you treat discipline as hatred. And then you start calling God "harsh" when He is actually being merciful.

Because conviction is the door to freedom.

But shame calls the door a threat.

So instead of walking through repentance, you retreat into secrecy. You start managing sin instead of forsaking it. You start adjusting language instead of changing life. You start calling darkness "struggle" so you don't have to call it sin.

And the longer shame rules, the more you lose your ability to hear correction without collapsing.

Because shame turns conviction into condemnation.

And when conviction becomes condemnation in your mind, repentance becomes impossible.

Shame Creates a Culture of Silence

Shame doesn't just imprison individuals.

It builds a culture.

A shame culture is when the house learns to protect appearances more than purity. People stop telling the truth because truth is punished. Confession feels dangerous. Correction feels "mean." And exposure gets labeled "division."

So everyone learns the same survival tactic:

Stay quiet.

Keep it hidden.

Don't bring it into the light.

That is not peace.

That is fear.

And fear is not the government of God.

Because the Kingdom does not grow in silence.

Freedom grows in light.

Scripture does not call hidden sin "wisdom." It calls it darkness. And it says light is what exposes it.

"But all things that are reproved are made manifest by the light…" (Ephesians 5:13, KJV)

Shame hates that verse.

Because shame survives on secrecy.

It needs you to believe that if something stays hidden, it stays safe. But hidden sin doesn't stay safe. It stays alive. It spreads. It contaminates. And it eventually becomes culture.

That is why shame cultures always produce the same fruit: people can sit in church while living double lives. Leaders can preach holiness while protecting compromise. Families can smile while wounds rot. And nobody speaks because speaking would expose what everyone is pretending not to see.

But God does not build houses on silence.

He builds houses on truth.

And truth requires light.

So here is the verdict: if a house calls exposure "attack," that house is being governed by shame, not by God.

Because shame creates silence.

And silence protects bondage.

Hardcore Example: Shame Tries to Veil the Glory

When the light shows up, shame doesn't celebrate.

Shame panics.

Because shame does not hate darkness.

Shame hates exposure.

Moses came down from the mountain and his face shone because he had been with God. The people saw it - and instead of running toward the presence, they recoiled from it.

Not because the glory was evil.

Because the glory revealed them.

"And it came to pass, when Moses came down from mount Sinai… that Moses wist not that the skin of his face shone… And when Aaron and all the children of Israel saw Moses, behold, the skin of his face shone; and they were afraid to come nigh him." (Exodus 34:29–30, KJV)

Read that again: afraid to come nigh him.

That is shame in its purest form.

Light is present.

But instead of repentance, the response is avoidance.

And what did they do next?

They demanded a covering.

They pressured Moses to veil what was exposing them - so they could stay comfortable without being changed.

"And till Moses had done speaking with them, he put a vail on his face." (Exodus 34:33, KJV) *"But when Moses went in before the LORD to speak with him, he took the vail off…"* (Exodus 34:34, KJV)

So the veil became a system: glory when Moses is with God, concealment when he is with the people.

That is what shame does in churches.

The house claims it wants God.

But when God gets close enough to expose mess, people start demanding a veil.

"Don't preach like that."

"Don't say it that strong."

"Don't confront that."

"Don't bring that up."

Not because it's unbiblical.

Because it's revealing.

And the New Testament doesn't soften this. It calls it what it is: a veil over the heart.

"But their minds were blinded… the vail is upon their heart." (2 Corinthians 3:14–15, KJV)

Shame wants the veil because a veil allows you to keep your reputation while avoiding repentance. It allows you to stay in the room while staying hidden. It allows you to say "I love God" while refusing the light of God.

But the Kingdom does not advance by veils.

It advances by turning.

"Nevertheless when it shall turn to the Lord, the vail shall be taken away." (2 Corinthians 3:16, KJV)

So here is the point of the example:

Shame doesn't just hide sin.

Shame tries to hide glory.

Because glory demands truth.

And truth demands repentance.

And shame would rather keep you comfortable than clean.

That is why shame builds a culture of silence.

It doesn't just tell you to cover your mess.

It tells the house to cover the light.

Shame Attacks Identity to Protect Bondage

Shame doesn't just say, "You did something wrong."

Shame says, "You are something wrong."

That is how it keeps people bound. Because if shame can attach sin to identity, you won't fight it like an enemy - you'll tolerate it like it's you.

So instead of saying, "I sinned," people start saying, "That's just who I am."

Instead of saying, "I need to repent," they say, "I'm broken."

Instead of saying, "Christ can change me," they say, "This is my struggle."

And that language sounds humble, but it's actually agreement with bondage.

Because the Kingdom does not call you by your wounds.

It calls you by your new birth.

Scripture says it plainly:

"Therefore if any man be in Christ, he is a new creature…" (2 Corinthians 5:17, KJV)

Shame hates that.

Because new creature language destroys old identity agreements.

Shame wants you to keep wearing the old name so the old chains stay legal. It wants you to keep calling yourself what you used to be so you never step into what Christ made you.

And this is where people get deceived: they think shame is "honesty." They think staying self-accusing is maturity. But self-accusation is not repentance. Repentance is turning.

And you cannot turn while you keep agreeing with the lie that you are permanently defined by your past.

Because shame attacks identity to protect bondage.

But Christ rebuilds identity to break bondage.

And the moment identity is restored, shame starts losing its grip - because shame cannot rule a person who believes what God says about them.

Shame Makes People Defend the Darkness

Shame doesn't just hide sin.

It defends it.

Because once a person has lived in secrecy long enough, the darkness becomes "protected territory." And when that territory is threatened by truth, shame does not respond with repentance.

It responds with excuses.

It responds with anger.

It responds with victim language.

It responds with blame.

Shame will make a person fight the very light that would heal them, because exposure feels like death to the false identity they've been maintaining.

So instead of saying, "You're right, I need to repent," they say, "You're judging me."

Instead of saying, "This is sin," they say, "You don't understand my situation."

Instead of saying, "God is correcting me," they say, "That's legalism."

And the moment those words come out, shame has accomplished its goal: it has turned light into an enemy.

But Scripture says the opposite. Light is how God rescues people. Light is how darkness loses its right to stay.

"And ye shall know the truth, and the truth shall make you free." (John 8:32, KJV)

Shame hates freedom.

Because freedom requires truth.

And truth requires exposure.

So shame trains people to defend the darkness with spiritual language - so they can stay bound while still appearing faithful.

That is why shame isn't just emotional pain.

It is a strategy.

And if you don't recognize it, you'll mistake defense for maturity, and excuses for wisdom.

But in the Kingdom, defense of darkness is rebellion.

Because shame makes people defend the darkness - and anything you defend, you keep.

Shame Blocks Repentance by Making Exposure Feel Fatal

Repentance is not complicated.

But shame makes it feel impossible.

Because repentance requires you to come into the light - and shame makes light feel like death.

Shame tells you exposure will destroy you.

Shame tells you confession will ruin you.

Shame tells you if people find out, you will be rejected forever.

So instead of repenting, you manage.

You adjust behavior just enough to stay hidden.

You change vocabulary.

You avoid accountability.

You stay in control.

But all of that is bondage with religious makeup.

Scripture does not treat confession as optional therapy.

It treats it as a doorway.

"If we confess our sins, he is faithful and just to forgive us our sins, and to cleanse us from all unrighteousness." (1 John 1:9, KJV)

Shame hates that verse because it destroys secrecy.

It says cleansing is tied to confession.

It says forgiveness is available.

It says cleansing is real.

But shame twists it. Shame whispers, "Yes, but not you. Not after what you did. Not after how long you've hidden. Not after how many times."

And that whisper is a lie.

Because shame is not the voice of God.

God corrects to restore.

Shame accuses to imprison.

So hear the line: shame blocks repentance by making exposure feel fatal.

But exposure is not your death.

Exposure is your rescue.

Because what stays hidden stays bound.

And what comes into the light can be cleansed.

The Blood Removes Guilt, and Truth Breaks Shame

Shame survives when people believe their sin is stronger than God's cleansing.

But the gospel does not offer "management."

It offers removal.

It offers cleansing.

It offers a conscience made clean.

Scripture says the blood of Christ doesn't just cover sin - it purges the conscience.

"How much more shall the blood of Christ… purge your conscience from dead works to serve the living God?" (Hebrews 9:14, KJV)

That is not poetic.

That is legal.

It means guilt loses its right to rule.

And when guilt loses its right to rule, shame loses its throne.

Because shame is guilt weaponized.

Shame is sin remembered without redemption applied.

So the blood deals with guilt, and truth deals with the lie shame told you about who you are.

That is why Scripture ties freedom to truth.

"And ye shall know the truth, and the truth shall make you free." (John 8:32, KJV)

Truth breaks the agreement.

Truth breaks the secrecy.

Truth breaks the false identity.

And once truth breaks shame, you don't have to live as a fig-leaf Christian. You can live clean. You can walk in light. You can be corrected without collapsing. You can be exposed without being destroyed - because Christ already carried the judgment your shame keeps threatening you with.

So hear this: the blood removes guilt, and truth breaks shame.

And when guilt and shame are dethroned, repentance becomes normal again.

Because you stop fearing exposure more than you fear bondage.

Shame Must Be Judged in the House

Shame is not a private issue.

Because a shame-governed house will always protect darkness. It will always punish confession. It will always reward silence. And it will always treat exposure like betrayal.

That is why shame must be judged.

Not "managed."

Judged.

Because judgment is a government act. It is the King saying, "This will not be allowed to rule here."

Scripture already established the pattern:

"For the time is come that judgment must begin at the house of God..." (1 Peter 4:17, KJV)

So when shame is tolerated in the house, the house becomes the safe place for hidden sin. People learn to perform. They learn to curate. They learn to stay quiet. And the house becomes full of fig leaves instead of cleansing.

But God does not fill what He does not govern.

And He will not walk in uncleanness.

He said it plainly: if the camp is unclean, He turns away.

"...therefore shall thy camp be holy: that he see no unclean thing in thee, and turn away from thee." (Deuteronomy 23:14, KJV)

So if a house wants the presence of God while tolerating shame culture, it is asking for glory while refusing government.

That will not work.

Shame must be judged in the house so truth can be normal, repentance can be safe, and cleansing can actually happen.

Because shame cannot rule where government is restored.

Conclusion: Shame Breaks When the Throne Is Restored

Shame rules wherever truth is unsafe.

Shame rules wherever confession is punished.

Shame rules wherever image matters more than purity.

And that is why shame has destroyed more people than open sin - because shame keeps people hiding while they keep bleeding.

But shame is not stronger than the gospel.

Shame is not stronger than the blood.

Shame is not stronger than truth.

The blood of Christ purges the conscience. (Hebrews 9:14)
Truth makes free. (John 8:32) And there is no condemnation in
Christ. (Romans 8:1)

Shame says, "You are something wrong."

Conviction says, "You did something wrong."

Shame attacks identity to keep bondage legal.

Conviction exposes sin so repentance can be real.

So shame only survives when you keep agreeing with it.

When you keep sewing fig leaves. (Genesis 3:7)

When you keep choosing silence. (Ephesians 5:13)

When you keep calling conviction condemnation.
(Hebrews 12:6)

When you keep defending darkness.

But shame breaks the moment the Throne is restored -
because shame cannot govern a person who is submitted to truth.
Shame cannot rule a house where repentance is normal. Shame
cannot survive where light is honored more than reputation.

So here is the conclusion:

Stop hiding.

Stop managing.

Stop sewing.

Come into the light.

Let God cleanse what you've protected.

Because shame is not your identity.

Shame is a thief.

And it breaks when the King is obeyed.

Scripture Index

Chapter Seven

False Authority Always Demands What God Never Did

Introduction: God Never Tests Sheep Like a Tyrant

God does not govern like insecurity.

He does not lead like fear.

He does not test people to satisfy suspicion.

He does not create pressure so leaders can feel in control.

That is not discernment.

That is not shepherding.

That is not government.

That is tyranny dressed in spiritual language.

One of the great corruptions in the Church is this: people have confused harshness with holiness, intimidation with authority, and control with leadership. They have been taught to call fear "submission" and silence "honor." But the Kingdom does not function by emotional hostage-taking. It functions by truth, order, righteousness, and the rule of Christ.

God never asked sheep to prove loyalty to a shepherd by violating conscience, ignoring fruit, or surrendering discernment. He never told leaders to invent tests He did not create. He never gave men permission to use pressure as proof of authority. He never authorized manipulation as a substitute for spiritual weight.

Scripture is plain:

"Neither as being lords over God's heritage, but being ensamples to the flock." (1 Peter 5:3, KJV)

That verse does not merely forbid bad tone.

It forbids illegitimate rule.

A shepherd is not a tyrant.

A shepherd is not a replacement throne.

A shepherd is not a jealous gatekeeper protecting personal control.

A shepherd is an under-shepherd.

That means he is under authority before he ever carries authority. It means he cannot command what Christ did not command. He cannot bind what Christ did not bind. He cannot demand what God never required.

And this is where false authority reveals itself. It always reaches beyond assignment. It always adds weight God did not place. It always creates standards that strengthen the leader instead of revealing the King.

Jesus did not build His Church on human domination. He built it on Himself.

"For other foundation can no man lay than that is laid, which is Jesus Christ." (1 Corinthians 3:11, KJV)

So this chapter must cut where many have been wounded and where many others have hidden ambition behind title. Because false authority does not merely bruise people. It distorts the image of God. It trains sheep to fear men. It teaches people to obey voices God never enthroned.

And where that is tolerated, the house becomes vulnerable to abuse, confusion, passivity, and corruption.

So the line must be drawn.

God never tests sheep like a tyrant.

And any authority that does is already speaking beyond its assignment.

Submission Is to God, Not Replaced Authority

Submission in the Kingdom is first upward.

It is to God.

It is to His Word.

It is to His government.

It is to His throne.

Everything else is secondary and derivative.

That is why the apostles answered so clearly:

"We ought to obey God rather than men." (Acts 5:29, KJV)

That is not rebellion.

That is order.

All human authority in the Kingdom is legitimate only while it remains under divine authority. The moment a leader demands what contradicts Scripture, competes with Christ, or seeks allegiance that belongs to God alone, that leader has stepped out of order. Submission to disorder is not virtue. It is participation in rebellion.

This is where many people have been trapped. They were told that questioning obvious compromise was dishonor. They were told that discerning fruit was rebellion. They were told that loyalty to a leader was the same as loyalty to Christ.

No.

Christ is not replaced by office.

Truth is not canceled by charisma.

Government is not transferred to personality.

Jesus said:

"But be not ye called Rabbi: for one is your Master, even Christ; and all ye are brethren." (Matthew 23:8, KJV)

That does not erase function.

It puts function in order.

There are leaders. There is oversight. There is accountability. There is government. But none of it exists to create a substitute Christ. None of it authorizes leaders to sit in the conscience of the saint and speak as though they are the final voice.

Real authority points upward.

False authority pulls inward.

Real authority says, "Obey God."

False authority says, "Prove yourself to me."

Real authority feeds the flock.

False authority feeds on the flock.

Real authority trembles at the Word.

False authority uses the Word to shield itself from exposure.

This is why the sheep must know the Shepherd.

"My sheep hear my voice, and I know them, and they follow me." (John 10:27, KJV)

Not every voice in a pulpit is His voice.

Not every demand made in ministry is from the throne.

Not every pressure is the Holy Ghost.

Submission is holy only when it remains ordered under Christ. When men replace that order, submission becomes distortion. The tragedy is that many sincere people stay trapped because they were taught to obey a structure instead of discerning whether the structure is still under God.

But the Kingdom never asks you to replace Jesus with a leader.

It asks leaders and sheep alike to bow to Jesus together.

Leaders Who Confuse Control With Government

Control is not government.

Control is fear trying to look strong.

Government carries clarity.

Control carries anxiety.

Government establishes boundaries because truth has them.

Control establishes pressure because insecurity needs it.

When leaders lose spiritual weight, they often compensate with force. They tighten the grip. They multiply requirements. They monitor, threaten, pressure, imply, and manipulate. They call it "covering." They call it "honor." They call it "alignment." But what they are really protecting is not the house. It is their own place in it.

That is why false authority often sounds intense, but it does not sound clean.

It constantly needs reassurance.

It constantly interprets disagreement as betrayal.

It constantly treats questions as threats.

It constantly confuses compliance with health.

But the Kingdom is not built on intimidation.

"The servant of the Lord must not strive; but be gentle unto all men, apt to teach, patient." (2 Timothy 2:24, KJV)

Gentleness is not weakness.

Patience is not compromise.

It is evidence that the leader is not trying to preserve control through flesh.

A leader under God does not need to manufacture fear to prove authority. Authority is already proven by alignment, fruit, truth, and spiritual weight.

Moses carried authority without self-promotion.

Samuel carried authority without manipulation.

Jesus carried absolute authority without carnality.

False authority cannot do that.

It depends on pressure because pressure becomes its counterfeit proof.

But Scripture describes real oversight this way:

"Feed the flock of God which is among you, taking the oversight thereof… not by constraint… neither as being lords over God's heritage, but being ensamples to the flock." (1 Peter 5:2–3, KJV)

Not by constraint.

That is a direct blow to control-based leadership.

If your leadership requires constant coercion, something deeper is broken. If the house is ruled by intimidation, public shaming, personal tests, selective access, emotional punishment, and implied rejection, that is not mature government. That is flesh trying to preserve power.

And flesh always overreaches.

Because it does not know how to govern.

It only knows how to grip.

Rejecting What God Sends Because of the Package

False authority does not only over-control.

It also misdiscerns.

Once leaders become attached to their own expectations, they start rejecting what God sends simply because it did not come wrapped in familiarity. They do not test by truth. They test by comfort. They do not weigh by Scripture. They weigh by preference. And when something from God disrupts their assumptions, they resist the package instead of discerning the source.

This has always been a problem.

Israel wanted a Messiah who matched natural expectation, and many missed Him because He did not arrive clothed in the form they preferred. (Isaiah 53:2–3; John 1:11)

The Pharisees claimed to protect truth, but they rejected Truth standing in front of them. Why? Because God had not submitted Himself to their format.

False authority still does that.

It rejects correction because the messenger is too young.

It rejects truth because the tone was not flattering.

It rejects warning because the vessel was not on the approved list.

It rejects people because they did not come through the channels insecurity prefers.

But God is not bound by human packaging.

"Judge not according to the appearance, but judge righteous judgment." (John 7:24, KJV)

That is not a call to naivety.

It is a call to spiritual discernment.

A house ruled by false authority becomes increasingly unable to receive from unexpected vessels. It can only receive what reinforces existing control. So it begins to filter truth through politics, relationships, personal preference, and internal loyalty systems.

And once that happens, the house is no longer being governed by truth.

It is being governed by culture.

That is dangerous.

Because God often sends what offends flesh before it heals the house. He often speaks through packages men would not have chosen. He often exposes corruption through voices that pride finds easy to dismiss.

So when leaders automatically reject what God sends because it does not look right to them, they are not protecting order.

They are protecting control.

And there is a difference.

Testing Loyalty Instead of Discerning Fruit

False authority loves loyalty tests.

Because loyalty tests let leaders measure devotion to themselves while pretending to guard the house.

But Scripture never tells shepherds to invent scenarios to see who is "with them." It tells leaders to discern fruit, weigh doctrine, and watch over souls under God. (Hebrews 13:17; 1 John 4:1)

Fruit is biblical.

Artificial testing is not.

"Ye shall know them by their fruits." (Matthew 7:16, KJV)

That means the Kingdom gives you a real standard.

Fruit.

Doctrine.

Character.

Obedience.

Endurance.

Holiness.

False authority replaces those with private games.

It withholds access to see who chases.

It creates confusion to see who stays quiet.

It sends mixed signals to see who remains emotionally dependent.

It invents conditions to prove submission.

That is not discernment.

That is manipulation.

And it always reveals fear.

Because secure authority does not need theater. It does not need hidden tests. It does not need psychological traps. It does not need to create uncertainty so people stay dependent. Truth is strong enough to stand in the open.

Paul did not tell the churches to prove loyalty to him through invented pressure. He said:

"Be ye followers of me, even as I also am of Christ." (1 Corinthians 11:1, KJV)

There is the standard.

Follow me as I follow Him.

That means the measure is never blind allegiance.

The measure is visible alignment.

The moment a leader wants to be followed beyond Christ, beyond Scripture, beyond righteousness, beyond accountability, that leader has crossed the line. And the sheep are not required to sanctify that violation with silence.

Loyalty is not proven by enduring abuse.

Loyalty is proven by remaining true to Christ.

Discernment asks, "What fruit is this producing?"

False authority asks, "How far will you go to prove you are mine?"

That is the wrong question.

No shepherd owns the sheep.

Abuse Thrives Where Authority Is Unchecked

Unchecked authority becomes a breeding ground.

When there is no accountability, no testing by Scripture, no courage in the sheep, and no humility in leadership, abuse does not remain an exception. It becomes a system. It learns the language of the house. It becomes normal. And once abuse becomes normal, truth begins to sound extreme.

That is how corruption settles in.

Ezekiel condemned shepherds who fed themselves instead of the flock:

"Woe be to the shepherds of Israel that do feed themselves! should not the shepherds feed the flocks?" (Ezekiel 34:2, KJV)

That indictment is still alive.

Any authority that consumes the weak, burdens the sincere, shields itself from correction, and manipulates access to preserve power is already moving in a corrupt pattern. Abuse may begin subtle. It may begin with atmosphere, implied threat, selective coldness, public pressure, spiritualized shame, or distorted "covering." But if it is left unchecked, it deepens.

Because sin always seeks structure.

That is why unchecked authority is so dangerous. It gives sin a system to live in. And once people learn that title is enough to silence questions, the door opens for deeper corruption.

This is why the sheep must not be trained into helplessness.

"Beloved, believe not every spirit, but try the spirits whether they are of God." (1 John 4:1, KJV)

An equipped people are harder to control.

A mature people are harder to deceive.

A governed people are less vulnerable to personality cults.

False authority thrives where saints are taught dependence instead of discernment.

It thrives where "peace" means silence.

It thrives where "honor" means immunity from correction.

It thrives where people fear men more than they fear God.

But God never intended the Church to function that way.

The house is safest when authority itself is under authority. The house is healthiest when leaders can be tested, corrected, weighed, and held to the same throne they preach. The house is strongest when no personality is allowed to rival Christ.

Because the moment unchecked authority is tolerated, the seeds of abuse are already present.

Conclusion - God Does Not Share His Throne

This is the final issue.

God does not share His throne.

Not with leaders.

Not with ministries.

Not with movements.

Not with personalities.

Not with systems that learned how to sound spiritual while remaining flesh-ruled.

Every false authority problem is, at root, a throne problem.

Someone wanted a place only Christ can hold.

Someone wanted an allegiance only God can require.

Someone wanted control that looked like government but was never submitted enough to carry it cleanly.

That is why false authority always demands what God never did.

It asks for unquestioned loyalty.

It asks for emotional dependence.

It asks for silence in the face of compromise.

It asks for submission beyond Scripture.

It asks sheep to protect the ego of the shepherd.

But God never asked for any of that.

He asked for obedience to Him.

He asked for holiness.

He asked for truth.

He asked for discernment.

He asked for shepherds to feed, guide, protect, and exemplify.

He did not authorize lordship over His inheritance. (1 Peter 5:3)

He did not authorize replacement thrones.

He did not authorize spiritual domination.

This is why false authority must be exposed without apology. Not because rebellion is being encouraged, but because true authority is being defended. Houses cannot hold glory while counterfeit government is enthroned. The River does not flow through manipulation. The weight of God does not rest where flesh is protected by title.

So the line is simple:

If it competes with Christ, reject it.

If it violates Scripture, refuse it.

If it protects abuse, expose it.

If it demands what God never commanded, it is false.

Because God does not share His throne.

And any leader who forgets that has already become dangerous.

Scripture Index

- 1 Corinthians 3:11
- Corinthians 11:1
- 1 Peter 5:2–3
- 1 Peter 5:3
- 1 John 4:1
- 2 Timothy 2:24
- Acts 5:29
- Ezekiel 34:2
- Hebrews 13:17
- Isaiah 53:2–3
- John 1:11
- John 7:24
- John 10:27
- Matthew 7:16
- Matthew 23:8

Chapter Eight

Obedience Is Not Optional

Introduction: Partial Obedience Is Still Disobedience

Obedience is not a preference. It is not a personality type. It is not a "mature believer" option you graduate into when you feel ready.

Obedience is the evidence that Jesus is Lord - because the moment He speaks, your will is no longer the highest authority in the room.

The Kingdom does not run on good intentions. It runs on commands.

That is why partial obedience is not "close enough." It is disobedience wearing religious clothing. It is the human heart trying to keep a corner of the throne while still claiming the benefits of submission.

And God will not share His throne.

You can weep and still resist. You can worship and still refuse. You can say "Lord" and still keep the final word for yourself.

"And why call ye me, Lord, Lord, and do not the things which I say?" (Luke 6:46, KJV)

Obedience is not about rule-keeping. It is about alignment. The command of God is not a suggestion offered for

151

consideration - it is the voice of government. When God speaks, He is not negotiating. He is establishing order. And when that order is rejected, everything downstream becomes unstable - authority, clarity, protection, even peace.

"If ye love me, keep my commandments." (John 14:15, KJV)

Here is the deception Babylon teaches: sacrifice can replace submission. That if you "give something" you can avoid obeying something. That an offering can cover a refusal. That pain can be a substitute for surrender.

But Scripture shuts that down with force.

"To obey is better than sacrifice, and to hearken than the fat of rams." (1 Samuel 15:22, KJV)

God does not reward what you chose to give when He already told you what to do.

Because sacrifice is what you select. Obedience is what you submit to.

And this is where the dividing line shows up: delayed obedience. People call it "processing." They call it "praying." They call it "waiting on confirmation." But when God has made it clear, delay is not neutral. Delay is the flesh trying to outlast the command.

Obedience does not require your comfort. It requires your death - your self-rule, your excuses, your private exceptions.

"Be ye doers of the word, and not hearers only, deceiving your own selves." (James 1:22, KJV)

This chapter is not here to motivate you. It is here to confront the part of you that still believes you can belong to the Kingdom while reserving the right to disagree with the King. The Kingdom is not built by admirers. It is built by the obedient.

And obedience is not optional.

Delayed Obedience Equals Refusal

Delayed obedience is not neutral.

It is not "wisdom." It is not "discernment." It is not "I'm just praying about it."

When God has made it clear, delay becomes a decision.

Delay is the flesh trying to buy time so the command will soften… or disappear… or be replaced by a more convenient version.

But God does not govern with suggestions.

He governs with words.

And the moment you delay what He said, you are revealing what is still sitting on your throne.

Because obedience has a timing.

If you obey later, you did not obey - you postponed.

And postponement is how rebellion hides in polite clothing.

"Therefore to him that knoweth to do good, and doeth it not, to him it is sin." (James 4:17, KJV)

Most people do not reject God with a clenched fist. They reject Him with a calendar.

They say, "Yes, Lord… but not yet."

And in the Kingdom, "not yet" is not agreement. It is refusal with a smile.

"Today if ye will hear his voice, harden not your hearts…" (Hebrews 3:15, KJV)

Notice what Scripture calls delay: a hardening.

Hardness is not only anger. Hardness is resistance.

Hardness is when you hear - and then you stall.

Hardness is when you know - and then you wait for a better option.

Hardness is when the command confronts your comfort and you begin to negotiate for a delay.

And that is exactly how people lose spiritual sensitivity: not with one dramatic rebellion, but with repeated small postponements.

The voice comes. The conviction comes. The instruction comes.

And the soul learns the pattern: "I can wait."

Then the next time God speaks, the response is weaker.

Not because God stopped speaking - but because you trained yourself to ignore His timing.

God Does Not Negotiate Commands

God does not negotiate commands.

He is not running a committee. He is not asking for feedback. He is not waiting for your comfort to catch up to His Lordship.

When God speaks, He is establishing government.

And the moment you treat a command like a suggestion, you are not "growing." You are resisting.

Obedience is not a spiritual accessory. It is the dividing line between self-rule and Kingdom rule.

"Not every one that saith unto me, Lord, Lord, shall enter into the kingdom of heaven; but he that doeth the will of my Father which is in heaven." (Matthew 7:21, KJV)

The Kingdom does not reward agreement in the mouth while rebellion stays in the will.

And this is where people misunderstand God: they think He measures sins like modern culture measures sins - by embarrassment level, by social cost, by public optics.

But Scripture measures by government.

Not "how bad did it look?" But "who did you obey?"

Idolatry → adultery → murder / covenant treason

Jesus did not present divorce as God's approval.

When they pressed Him about divorce, He said Moses *permitted* it "because of the hardness of your hearts" - and then He drew a hard boundary: *"from the beginning it was not so."* (Matthew 19:8, KJV)

That means divorce is not God's design. It is what hardness produces.

And Jesus takes it back to covenant government:

"For this cause shall a man leave father and mother, and shall cleave to his wife: and they twain shall be one flesh… What therefore God hath joined together, let not man put asunder." (Matthew 19:5–6, KJV)

One flesh is joining. Union. Covenant.

And Scripture makes something else just as clear: sexual sin is not merely behavior - it is joining.

"What? know ye not that he which is joined to an harlot is one body? for two, saith he, shall be one flesh." (1 Corinthians 6:16, KJV)

So adultery is not just "a mistake." It is covenant betrayal. It is joining yourself outside the covenant and tearing what God joined. It destroys what marriage is meant to protect - union, trust, covenant covering.

And that is why Jesus says unlawful divorce and remarriage functions as adultery. (Matthew 5:31–32)

Now hear the point with weight: when covenant is torn, something dies.

Adultery murders covenant.

Not always with a knife - but with betrayal.

It kills what was joined. It kills intimacy. It kills trust. It kills the "one flesh" reality God established.

And idolatry is the same rebellion wearing spiritual language.

God describes His relationship with His people in covenant terms - like marriage. He calls Himself a husband to His people. (Jeremiah 3:14) And the New Covenant reveals the Church as the Bride, joined to Christ. (Ephesians 5:31–32; Revelation 19:7)

So when you worship an idol, you are not just "distracted." You are covenant unfaithful.

"Ye adulterers and adulteresses, know ye not that the friendship of the world is enmity with God?" (James 4:4, KJV)

Spiritual adultery is not a metaphor meant to be cute. It is Heaven's accusation: divided loyalty is betrayal.

And betrayal murders covenant.

So when you put it together, you see why Scripture treats idolatry, adultery, and murder with the same seriousness: they are all covenant-level treason.

Different expressions. Same root.

Self-rule against God's throne.

Under the Law, murder carried public judgment. (Exodus 21:12) Adultery carried public judgment. (Leviticus 20:10) Idolatry carried public judgment as covenant treason. (Deuteronomy 13:6–10)

God was not "grading" them differently as if one was harmless. He was exposing that they all strike the same thing: covenant government.

Because the question is not, "Did you slip?" The question is, "Who did you join yourself to?"

When you were called to belong to God, you were called to be His. When you were called to Christ, you were called to union.

And union does not tolerate rivals.

That's why obedience is not optional. Because disobedience is not merely an act - it is allegiance.

"He that is not with me is against me…" (Matthew 12:30, KJV)

The Kingdom does not make room for private exceptions. It does not honor "mostly submitted." It does not reward "I obey in the areas I agree with."

A King is not King where His commands can be rejected.

So the call of this chapter is simple and violent against the flesh:

Stop negotiating. Stop delaying. Stop dressing refusal in spiritual language.

If He is Lord, obey Him.

"If ye love me, keep my commandments." (John 14:15, KJV)

Sacrifice Is Not a Substitute for Submission

Sacrifice is what you choose.

Obedience is what God commands.

And the human heart loves sacrifice - because sacrifice feels powerful while still letting you keep control. You can give something and still protect something. You can offer what you're willing to release while refusing what God actually targeted.

But God does not accept substitutes.

He does not take offerings as payment to ignore disobedience.

"Behold, to obey is better than sacrifice, and to hearken than the fat of rams." (1 Samuel 15:22, KJV)

That verse is not poetic.

It is a verdict.

Because the problem is never that people give nothing. The problem is that people give what they prefer instead of obeying what they were told.

And the moment you do that, sacrifice becomes a mask.

A mask for rebellion. A mask for delay. A mask for self-rule.

Some people "serve" to avoid surrender. Some people "give" to avoid obeying. Some people "worship" to avoid repentance.

They stay busy so they don't have to bow.

But God sees straight through it.

"He hath shewed thee, O man, what is good; and what doth the LORD require of thee, but to do justly, and to love mercy, and to walk humbly with thy God?" (Micah 6:8, KJV)

Humility is not tone.

Humility is submission.

And submission is proven by obedience - especially when it costs you something you wanted to keep.

Because in the Kingdom, the command is not merely instruction.

It is government.

So when the command comes and you offer sacrifice instead, you are doing something deeper than "missing a step."

You are telling Heaven: I will decide what I give, not You.

And that is not devotion.

That is idolatry of the will.

Now watch how this shows up in real life.

God tells a man to repent, but he increases his church activity. God tells a woman to forgive, but she "fasts" while keeping bitterness. God calls a leader to correct sin, but he gives money instead - hoping generosity will replace righteousness.

But the Kingdom does not accept bribery dressed as worship.

"Bring no more vain oblations…" (Isaiah 1:13, KJV)

God called offerings "vain" when the heart refused obedience.

Not because God hates giving - He commands giving. But because He refuses a sacrifice that is meant to replace submission.

That is why the Bible repeatedly connects sacrifice to a life that is aligned.

"I beseech you therefore, brethren… that ye present your bodies a living sacrifice… which is your reasonable service." (Romans 12:1, KJV)

Living sacrifice is not money.

It is you.

Your will on the altar. Your pride on the altar. Your private exceptions on the altar.

Because God is not after what you can donate.

He is after who you are willing to obey.

"If any man will come after me, let him deny himself, and take up his cross, and follow me." (Matthew 16:24, KJV)

You cannot follow while negotiating.

You cannot carry a cross and keep your throne.

So hear it clean:

Sacrifice is not the price you pay to keep disobedience.

Sacrifice is the evidence that obedience already took place.

Because in the Kingdom, obedience is not optional - and sacrifice without obedience is just religion trying to stay in control.

Vision Without Government Becomes Idolatry

People love the word *vision* because it sounds spiritual while still leaving them in charge.

But vision without government is not leadership. It is self-rule wearing prophetic vocabulary.

The Kingdom is not built by what you "see." It is built by what you obey.

"And why call ye me, Lord, Lord, and do not the things which I say?" (Luke 6:46, KJV)

Here is the trap: a person can become so committed to what they believe they are called to do that they stop submitting to what God is commanding them to do. And when that happens, the "vision" becomes the authority. The "vision" becomes the justification. The "vision" becomes the idol.

And then everything bends around it - people, relationships, conscience, Scripture itself.

That is how Babylon operates: it convinces you that being *driven* is the same thing as being *submitted.*

But Scripture exposes the real root:

"There is a way which seemeth right unto a man, but the end thereof are the ways of death." (Proverbs 14:12, KJV)

When you are ruled by what "seems right," you are not under government - you are under self.

And self-government always produces the same fruit:

"In those days there was no king in Israel: every man did that which was right in his own eyes." (Judges 21:25, KJV)

No king means no restraint. No king means no correction. No king means no accountability.

So people chase outcomes and call it "purpose," while ignoring commands and calling it "process."

But Jesus did not say, "My sheep are the ones with the biggest plans." He said:

"My sheep hear my voice, and I know them, and they follow me." (John 10:27, KJV)

Following is obedience. Hearing is submission. That is government.

And the moment you treat instruction as optional, you are no longer following the Shepherd - you are leading yourself.

That is why vision cannot be trusted unless it is under obedience. If the "vision" requires you to bypass commands, override conscience, trample covenant, or excuse rebellion, it is not vision from God - it is an idol demanding worship.

Obedience Is Proof of Alignment

Obedience is not a personality trait. It is alignment made visible.

Alignment is not what you claim. Alignment is what you submit to when the command touches what you love.

"Can two walk together, except they be agreed?" (Amos 3:3, KJV)

Agreement in the Kingdom is not mental assent. It is directional surrender. If God says *move*, alignment moves. If God says *stop*, alignment stops. If God says *cut it off*, alignment does not negotiate for a safer version of holiness.

This is why obedience is the proof of spiritual government. When your life is aligned, Heaven's order flows through you. When your life is divided, authority leaks.

"If a man love me, he will keep my words..." (John 14:23, KJV)

Jesus ties love to obedience because love is not measured by intensity - love is measured by loyalty. And loyalty is measured by compliance.

That is why Scripture connects hearing to doing, not hearing to admiring:

"But be ye doers of the word, and not hearers only, deceiving your own selves." (James 1:22, KJV)

Deception is not always believing a lie out there. Sometimes deception is believing you are submitted because you are informed.

Information without obedience does not produce alignment. It produces a religious conscience with no government.

And the moment God speaks into a specific area - money, sexuality, bitterness, pride, gossip, secret compromise - obedience becomes the test that exposes what you are truly aligned to.

"No man can serve two masters..." (Matthew 6:24, KJV)

You don't need to wonder if you're aligned.

Look at what you obey.

Because alignment is not proven in the areas you like. Alignment is proven in the areas that cost you.

Selective Obedience Restricts Authority

Selective obedience always produces restricted authority.

Because authority is not a title you claim. Authority is a weight God entrusts - where alignment can hold it.

"He that is faithful in that which is least is faithful also in much..." (Luke 16:10, KJV)

If you will not obey in the "least," you cannot be trusted with "much." Not because God is petty - because government is real. A divided vessel cannot carry undivided power.

This is the deception: people want Kingdom results while reserving private exceptions.

They want peace without repentance. They want authority without submission. They want anointing without alignment.

But the Kingdom does not run that way.

"For rebellion is as the sin of witchcraft, and stubbornness is as iniquity and idolatry..." (1 Samuel 15:23, KJV)

Rebellion is not merely "disagreement." It is spiritual resistance. It is refusal of government. And stubbornness - holding your ground against God - Scripture calls it idolatry because you have enthroned your will.

That is why partial obedience is not safe. It trains the soul to live with two thrones: one public, one private.

And private exceptions eventually become public fruit.

A person who is selectively obedient will eventually become selectively truthful. Selectively accountable. Selectively repentant.

And wherever selective obedience exists, confusion grows - because people no longer know what voice actually carries weight: God's voice, or the leader's preferences.

"If any man will do his will, he shall know of the doctrine…" (John 7:17, KJV)

Jesus ties knowing to doing. Many people want certainty without obedience. But clarity comes through compliance. When you obey, you sharpen discernment. When you resist, you dull it.

So hear it plain:

If you want increased authority, stop asking God for more power while protecting disobedience. Close the leaks. Submit fully. Obey quickly. Align completely.

Because God does not pour weight into vessels that refuse government.

Hard Core Biblical Example: When a Corrupt Voice Rewrites a Clear Command

Illustration: An Older Prophet Can Still Be a Lying Voice

There is a brutal story in Scripture that many would rather soften because it strikes too close to the structure of religious sabotage.

God sent a young prophet with a clear command. The assignment was plain. The word was plain. The boundary was plain. He was to go, deliver the word of the Lord, and leave without turning aside.

"For so was it charged me by the word of the Lord, saying, Eat no bread, nor drink water, nor turn again by the same way that thou camest." (1 Kings 13:9)

That was not vague.

That was not symbolic.

That was not "open to interpretation."

That was a command.

And when God gives a command, the future of the assignment is tied to the obedience of the servant.

But then another voice appeared.

Not a pagan voice.

Not a secular voice.

Not an open enemy.

An older prophet.

A recognized voice.

A spiritual man with prophetic history.

A man who knew the language, knew the culture, knew how to sound believable, and knew exactly how to override the younger prophet's guard.

That is what makes the story so violent.

The greatest danger did not come from an obvious enemy.

It came through a trusted spiritual voice.

The older prophet said, in effect, "You can come with me. The command has changed. I have new revelation. I have an angelic update. I know what God said to you, but here is what God is saying now."

And Scripture does not leave the matter unclear.

"He said unto him, I am a prophet also as thou art; and an angel spake unto me by the word of the Lord, saying, Bring him back with thee into thine house, that he may eat bread and drink water. But he lied unto him." (1 Kings 13:18)

But he lied unto him.

There it is.

No softer wording.

No religious padding.

No diplomatic reinterpretation.

He lied.

A mature voice lied.

A prophetic voice lied.

An older prophet lied.

And the younger prophet died.

That story is not only about obedience.

It is also about corruption in mentorship.

It is about the sabotage of a false or compromised older voice.

It is about what happens when a younger vessel abandons what God clearly said because a more established voice contradicted it.

And this still happens.

It happens when leaders full of pride cannot celebrate what is rising under them.

It happens when jealous men smile in public and sabotage in private.

It happens when tyranny learns how to speak in the accent of fathering.

It happens when compromised mentors rewrite clear commands in the name of wisdom, balance, timing, process, culture, loyalty, or submission.

And then when the damage is done, some of them dare to call it testing.

It is not testing.

It is sabotage.

It is not fathering.

It is corruption.

It is not protection.

It is a lying spirit using rank, familiarity, and misplaced trust to wound the future of the house.

The younger prophet was not destroyed because God was unclear.

He was destroyed because he let a secondary voice override the primary word.

That is why this story is terrifying. Many rising people are not destroyed first by lust, money, or open rebellion. Many are destroyed because they trust a voice with history more than the word with clarity.

And after the prophet disobeyed, judgment came.

"And when he was gone, a lion met him by the way, and slew him." (1 Kings 13:24)

That is severe.

Because Heaven was showing that disobedience does not become safe because it was suggested by someone spiritual.

A corrupt older voice does not lessen the danger of rebellion.

It multiplies it.

This is where the spirit of Balaam enters the discussion.

Balaam did not always attack God's people by direct assault. He corrupted them by counsel. He taught seduction. He taught compromise. He taught how to make a holy people fall by creating unlawful agreement.

Scripture says Balaam caused Israel to stumble.

"And Israel abode in Shittim, and the people began to commit whoredom with the daughters of Moab. And they called the people unto the sacrifices of their gods: and the people did eat, and bowed down to their gods." (Numbers 25:1–2)

Later Scripture exposes the root behind it:

"Behold, these caused the children of Israel, through the counsel of Balaam, to commit trespass against the Lord in the matter of Peor..." (Numbers 31:16)

That is the Balaam pattern.

Not always open cursing.

Corrupt counsel.

Not always direct attack.

Strategic seduction.

Not always obvious war.

Subtle compromise introduced through influence.

And Jesus says that spirit can sit inside a church.

"But I have a few things against thee, because thou hast there them that hold the doctrine of Balaam, who taught Balac to cast a stumblingblock before the children of Israel, to eat things sacrificed unto idols, and to commit fornication." (Revelation 2:14)

Notice the language.

Doctrine of Balaam.

That means this is not merely a personality flaw.

It is a pattern.

It is a teaching spirit.

It is a corrupt influence that trains people to violate boundaries, normalize mixture, and stumble into judgment while still feeling spiritual.

That is why the older prophet in 1 Kings 13 fits the same dark pattern. He became a stumbling voice. He used spiritual credibility to move a younger prophet off a clear command. He rewrote a boundary God had established. He became the kind of mentor whose influence does not preserve the future but damages it.

And this still happens in churches.

A leader sees grace on a younger vessel and instead of protecting it, begins controlling it.

Instead of strengthening it, he confuses it.

Instead of clarifying the word of the Lord, he muddies it.

Instead of guarding the future, he wounds it.

Some do this out of jealousy.

Some out of insecurity.

Some out of pride.

Some because they are tyrants and cannot tolerate a voice they do not own.

Some because they are compromised and know a truly obedient vessel will eventually expose the rot in the house.

So they interfere.

They delay.

They contradict.

They smother.

They introduce unlawful counsel.

They call compromise wisdom.

They call fear discernment.

They call sabotage testing.

But they are not testing sons.

They are destroying future leaders.

And when leaders do this, they do not merely wound individuals.

They injure the body.

They damage trust.

They harm the Kingdom witness.

They teach a generation to doubt both authority and prophecy because corrupt voices made obedience dangerous.

That is why Romans 13:14 belongs here with force.

"But put ye on the Lord Jesus Christ, and make not provision for the flesh, to fulfil the lusts thereof." (Romans 13:14)

Provision is agreement made practical.

Provision is what happens when a lie is given room.

Provision is what happens when a corrupt leader opens a door that God had shut.

Provision is what happens when a younger servant makes space for a voice God never authorized to rewrite the command.

And once provision is made, destruction is not far behind.

This is why the lesson must be stated with severity:

An older prophet can still be a lying voice.

A mature leader can still be corrupt.

A mentor can still be full of pride.

A recognized voice can still be carrying Balaam's counsel.

And no title, history, gift, or age gives a man the right to rewrite what God already said.

If God spoke clearly, then every later voice must bow to that word.

If a leader contradicts what God commanded, that leader is not functioning as protection.

That leader is functioning as danger.

And some of the deepest wounds in the body of Christ have come not from open enemies, but from trusted voices who used influence to redirect obedience and then called the wreckage "process."

No.

Call it what Scripture calls it.

He lied unto him. (1 Kings 13:18)

That is why obedience cannot be outsourced.

Discernment cannot be surrendered.

And loyalty cannot be given to a leader at the expense of what God already said.

Because when a corrupt voice rewrites a clear command, the issue is no longer mere counsel.

It is war against the future.

Conclusion: Obedience Is Not Optional

Obedience is not optional because Jesus is not a suggestion.

If He is Lord, then His voice is government. If His voice is government, then delay is refusal. If delay is refusal, then partial obedience is still disobedience.

And if obedience is treated as optional, you are not building the Temple - you are building a religious structure that cannot hold Glory.

This chapter has exposed the root: rebellion is not mainly behavior. Rebellion is allegiance. It is who you obey when the command collides with your comfort.

That is why Scripture treats covenant betrayal with severity - because idolatry, adultery, and murder are different fruits of the same thing: self-rule against God's throne.

So the call is not complicated:

Stop negotiating with God. Stop delaying what He already said. Stop offering sacrifice as a substitute for submission.

Obey - quickly, fully, and without private exceptions.

Because the Kingdom does not belong to admirers. It belongs to the obedient.

Scripture Index

- Amos 3:3
- Exodus 20:3–5

- Exodus 21:12
- Galatians 5:16

- Hebrews 3:15
- Isaiah 1:13
- James 1:22
- James 4:4
- Jeremiah 3:14
- John 7:17
- John 10:27
- John 14:15
- John 14:23
- Judges 21:25
- Luke 6:46
- Luke 16:10
- Matthew 5:21–22
- Matthew 5:31–32
- Matthew 6:24
- Matthew 7:21
- Matthew 12:30
- Matthew 16:24
- Matthew 19:5–8
- Micah 6:8
- Proverbs 14:12
- Revelation 19:7
- Romans 12:1
- 1 Corinthians 6:16
- 1 Samuel 15:22–23
- Leviticus 20:10
- Deuteronomy 13:6–10

Chapter Nine

Trust Restored

Introduction: Authority Is Weight, Not Permission

Authority in the Kingdom is not permission to act - it is weight assigned to govern. It is not given to validate identity, affirm calling, or reward ambition. Authority exists to protect people, preserve order, and sustain what God is building. That is why authority is never casual in Scripture, and why God is never hurried to restore it once it has been fractured.

Modern leadership culture treats authority as a platform - something to stand on, speak from, and be seen through. The Kingdom treats authority as a burden - something that presses on the soul, exposes the spine, and reveals what has been quietly forming beneath the surface. Authority tests a person more than it empowers them. It does not change who someone is; it reveals who they already are.

This chapter segment establishes a foundation the Church routinely ignores: trust comes before weight. *"He that is faithful in that which is least is faithful also in much"* (Luke 16:10, KJV). The Kingdom does not measure readiness by excitement, charisma, or vision language. God measures stewardship - endurance, restraint, and consistency over time.

Trust Is the True Measure of Readiness

Trust is not a feeling. Trust is not a calling. Trust is not confidence, charisma, gifting, passion, or intensity. Trust is a measurement. God does not ask whether someone feels ready; He measures whether someone has been faithful. Readiness in the Kingdom is never declared by desire or vision language. It is revealed by endurance, restraint, and consistency over time.

Scripture never elevates gifting as the qualification for responsibility. Gifting attracts attention; faithfulness governs authority. The Kingdom of God does not operate on excitement cycles, emotional momentum, or personality-driven leadership. It operates on stewardship. Where faithfulness is absent, authority becomes dangerous because power amplifies what character cannot restrain.

"Moreover it is required in stewards, that a man be found faithful." (1 Corinthians 4:2, KJV)

Faithfulness leaves evidence. It produces a trail that can be examined. Trust is built when obedience continues without recognition, when alignment remains under pressure, and when submission persists even when correction feels unfair. Anyone can obey when watched. Few obey when unseen. That difference determines whether authority can be entrusted safely.

One of the most damaging assumptions in church leadership is the belief that repentance automatically restores trust. Repentance restores relationship; it does not automatically restore government. Government carries consequences beyond the individual. When authority is re-released prematurely, the house pays the price for the leader's healing process.

Jesus never said passion qualifies a person for more. He never said gifting qualifies a person for weight. He said faithfulness does. Faithfulness proves that power will be stewarded rather than exploited, that authority will protect rather than dominate, and that responsibility will not be used to shield insecurity.

"He that is faithful in that which is least is faithful also in much." (Luke 16:10, KJV)

Small assignments are not insignificant to God; they are examinations. They reveal whether authority will be carried or corrupted. What many dismiss as beneath them, God uses as a measuring rod. The Kingdom does not test people with crowds first - it tests them with constraints. Until faithfulness is proven in the unseen, authority is withheld - not as punishment, but as mercy to the individual and protection for the house.

Trust is rebuilt slowly because trust is fragile. It is not restored by apology, but by pattern. It is not regained by tears, but by time. When trust returns, authority can follow. When trust does not return, authority must remain withheld - no matter how gifted, sincere, or anointed someone appears.

Authority Always Follows Proven Stewardship

In the Kingdom of God, authority never precedes stewardship - it follows it. Authority is not granted because someone is gifted, visible, or persuasive. It is granted because someone has demonstrated the capacity to carry responsibility without abusing it. Stewardship is the proving ground where motives are exposed long before authority magnifies them.

God does not entrust weight to untested hands because weight reveals structure. Before authority is released publicly, stewardship is proven privately. Scripture consistently ties rulership to faithfulness over time, not to sudden momentum or perceived potential.

"Well done, thou good and faithful servant: thou hast been faithful over a few things, I will make thee ruler over many things." (Matthew 25:21, KJV)

Notice the order. Faithfulness comes first. Rulership follows. Authority is never the training ground - it is the test result. When leaders attempt to reverse this order, authority becomes destructive instead of protective.

Stewardship exposes motive long before authority exposes character. Those who resent small responsibility reveal insecurity. Those who chafe under oversight reveal unresolved pride. Those who demand position before proving restraint reveal ambition that has not yet been crucified. God does not ignore these signals. He measures them carefully.

One of the clearest patterns in Scripture is that God entrusts process before power. Moses stewarded sheep before stewarding a nation. David stewarded obscurity before stewarding Israel. Joseph stewarded integrity in confinement before stewarding authority in government. In every case, God watched how they handled what could not exalt them before He entrusted them with what could.

This is why impatience is such a dangerous indicator in leadership. Impatience reveals a desire for influence without the burden of responsibility. Stewardship, by contrast, teaches restraint. It trains a person to carry obligation without applause and accountability without authority. Only those who learn that discipline can safely govern others.

Jesus Himself modeled this principle. Though He was the Son, He did nothing outside alignment with the Father (John 5:19). Authority flowed from submission, not independence. That pattern has never changed.

Stewardship also reveals how a person treats people when there is nothing to gain. Do they use others to advance themselves, or do they serve others even when service delays their own advancement? Authority entrusted to someone who has not learned to serve will always become a tool for self-preservation.

Many leadership failures occur not because authority was given, but because it was given too soon. When stewardship is bypassed, authority becomes unstable. When stewardship is honored, authority becomes safe. God delays authority not to frustrate leaders, but to protect people.

It is important to understand that stewardship is not merely about tasks; it is about trustworthiness under constraint. Can someone remain aligned when their opinion is overruled? Can they remain faithful when correction is uncomfortable? Can they remain obedient when their gifting is underutilized? These questions determine readiness far more than any résumé or testimony.

This is why God often entrusts leaders with responsibility that feels limiting before He entrusts them with authority that feels expansive. Limits reveal whether a person can govern themselves. Until self-government is proven, external government must remain limited.

Authority that arrives before stewardship is always borrowed - it has no roots. Authority that follows stewardship is grounded, resilient, and able to withstand pressure. God builds leaders the same way He builds houses: foundation first, weight later.

Why God Releases Authority Gradually

God restores authority gradually, not because He is hesitant, but because authority is not neutral. Authority is a force that reveals, not heals. When placed on a person too quickly, it does not strengthen weak areas - it exposes them. This is why God does not rush restoration and why impatience around authority is often a warning sign rather than a virtue.

In Scripture, authority is never used as therapy. It is never given to fix insecurity, heal wounds, or stabilize identity. Authority magnifies whatever already exists. Where humility is present, authority deepens it. Where pride is present, authority accelerates it. Where discernment is weak, authority makes the weakness visible to everyone.

This is why God often withholds authority even after repentance has occurred. Government affects others. When authority is released prematurely, the cost is not paid by the leader alone. When authority is released prematurely, the cost is not paid by the leader alone - it is paid by the house.

One of the most uncomfortable truths revealed in Scripture is that God does not only discipline leaders by removing authority. Many times, He disciplines leaders by allowing them to retain or exercise authority long enough to expose themselves. In other words, promotion itself can become judgment.

When leaders resist correction, dismiss counsel, or trust their own discernment above God's order, the Lord may step back - not to endorse their decisions, but to allow authority to reveal what correction could have healed.

"If the blind lead the blind, both shall fall into the ditch." (Matthew 15:14, KJV)

This is not accidental. It is intentional restraint on God's part.

Rehoboam is the clearest example. He rejected seasoned counsel and elevated voices that affirmed his pride. Scripture does not say God tried to stop him. It says the outcome was from the Lord.

"So the king hearkened not unto the people; for the cause was from the LORD." (1 Kings 12:15, KJV)

That statement is terrifying if taken seriously. God did not intervene to correct the decision. He allowed it to proceed so that the character of the leader would be fully exposed. The promotion of the wrong counsel became the mechanism of judgment. What humility could have prevented, authority made public.

This pattern appears repeatedly. Saul's authority did not heal his insecurity; it exposed it. His promotions, appointments, and decisions increasingly reflected fear rather than obedience. Authority did not stabilize Saul - it destabilized the kingdom. God allowed it to continue until the evidence was undeniable (1 Sam 15).

This is why God restores authority slowly. Gradual restoration protects the house and reveals whether correction has actually taken root. Time allows fruit to appear. Quick restoration masks problems. Slow restoration exposes them.

Another difficult truth must be stated plainly: many leaders are disciplined by being allowed to promote the wrong people.

God will permit a leader to elevate those who reflect their blind spots in order to expose the leader's lack of discernment. The punishment is not external - it is self-inflicted. Authority becomes the mirror.

Biblical Example - Saul Promotes the Wrong Man

Scripture gives a sobering example of a leader being judged through the very person he empowered. King Saul did not merely fail through disobedience; he failed through discernment. When Saul's insecurity hardened into paranoia, he surrounded himself not with righteous counsel, but with those willing to carry out his fear.

Doeg the Edomite was not a priest. He was not a covenant insider. He was a foreigner positioned close to Saul's authority. Scripture tells us Saul placed him over his servants, giving him proximity and influence he should never have had (1 Samuel 22:9).

When Saul ordered the priests of the Lord executed, his own guards refused. They feared God more than the king. But the man Saul had elevated had no such restraint.

"And the king said to Doeg, Turn thou, and fall upon the priests. And Doeg the Edomite turned, and he fell upon the priests, and slew on that day fourscore and five persons that did wear a linen ephod." (1 Samuel 22:18, KJV)

Saul did not wield the sword himself - his promotion did. The judgment against Saul was executed through the very man he empowered. God did not stop the appointment. God allowed the promotion to reveal the king's heart and the cost of his leadership.

This was discipline by permission. Saul's lack of discernment was exposed publicly, and innocent blood was shed because authority was placed in the wrong hands. The promotion became the punishment.

Scripture later records that Doeg's actions were remembered by God and condemned (Psalm 52). But the greater indictment fell on Saul - because leaders are responsible not only for what they do, but for who they empower.

This pattern has never changed. When leaders refuse correction, God may allow them to elevate those who reflect their fears, pride, or ambition. The leader's authority becomes the instrument of exposure. What humility could have prevented, promotion makes irreversible.

This is why some collapses seem preventable in hindsight. They were. Correction was offered. Counsel was available. But when leaders reject restraint, God may allow authority to finish the lesson.

"Before destruction the heart of man is haughty, and before honour is humility." (Proverbs 18:12, KJV)

God's gradual process is not cruelty; it is mercy. It gives leaders space to align before authority magnifies misalignment. When authority is restored slowly, humility has time to deepen, discernment has time to sharpen, and obedience has time to stabilize.

For the humble, gradual restoration is protection. For the proud, sudden authority is exposure.

And in both cases, God remains just.

The House Pays for the Leader's Discernment

Authority never stays private. The moment weight is placed on a leader, it affects everyone connected to that leader - every decision, every promotion, every silence, every compromise. That is why God restores authority slowly. He is not only restoring a person; He is protecting a house.

This section has exposed a hard Kingdom reality: leaders are tested not only by what they do, but by who they elevate. Promotion reveals what a leader values. It reveals whether character is honored or loyalty is preferred. It reveals whether government is intact or whether insecurity is steering the throne.

Saul proves it. Authority did not heal him - it exposed him. And once his government collapsed, he empowered the wrong man. When righteous men refused to comply, Saul found someone who would do what conscience would not. That is how a kingdom destabilizes: not with one loud rebellion, but with a leader whose discernment is broken and whose promotions become perverse.

So hear the warning and the pattern: God does not re-release weight to houses that cannot carry it. If trust is not rebuilt, authority becomes a weapon. If discernment is not healed, promotion becomes judgment. And when promotion becomes judgment, the house pays for what the leader refused to correct.

Trust comes before weight. Government comes before platform. And when God restores authority, He does it to protect the people - not to satisfy the leader.

Conclusion: Trust Determines Access to Authority

Authority is not restored because someone wants it back. Authority is restored because trust has made it safe again.

That is the verdict.

Not gifting. Not charisma. Not intensity. Not desire. Trust.

Because authority is weight, not permission. It is never released to satisfy ambition, reward longing, or validate calling language. It is released where stewardship has been proven, where discernment has been tested, and where the house will not be forced to suffer for a leader's instability.

This is why God moves slowly with authority.

He is not delaying out of cruelty. He is protecting what weight will touch.

Trust is the true measure of readiness because trust reveals what gifting cannot. Gifting can attract attention. Gifting can create momentum. Gifting can make people appear powerful before they are safe. But trust reveals whether the person can carry weight without abusing it, whether they can remain aligned without visibility, and whether authority will protect the house rather than expose it to unnecessary damage.

That is why authority always follows proven stewardship. God does not place weight on unstable hands. He does not hurry leaders into responsibility because they appear sincere. He measures what remains under pressure. He watches what happens in hidden places. He tests whether the person can carry small responsibility without private exception before larger weight is ever considered.

And this is why discernment matters so much.

Saul did not only fail by disobedience. He failed by promotion.

He empowered the wrong man, and the house paid for it. The judgment was not only in what Saul did himself, but in what his discernment released into the structure. That is the warning: authority never stays private. Every wrong promotion, every tolerated blind spot, every insecure elevation eventually reaches the house.

So let the issue be settled.

Authority is not a right. It is a trust.

And where trust has not been rebuilt, authority must remain withheld. Not as rejection, but as protection. Because in the Kingdom, trust determines access to authority

Chapter Ten

Authority Tested

Introduction: Visibility Is Not Proof of Government

A platform is not government. A microphone is not authority. Visibility is not weight. Momentum is not trust.

In the Kingdom, authority is never proved by how many people listen. It is proved by whether heaven can entrust you with weight without you turning that weight into self. That is why God tests leadership long before He expands it. He examines what rises in a person when influence increases, what awakens when access is granted, and what takes the throne when the room starts calling someone "anointed."

This chapter is about the test.

Not the gift. Not the calling language. The test.

Saul is the warning: authority does not heal insecurity - it exposes it. And once government collapses in the heart, it eventually collapses in the house. Promotions become perverse. Discernment fractures. Righteous men refuse what conscience will not allow, and the leader finds a Doeg - someone willing to do what faithful servants will not do.

This is why God tests authority before He enlarges it. The real question is not whether a leader can speak. The question is whether a leader can be governed - whether hidden places remain clean, whether self-rule dies under pressure, and whether weight can be carried without building a personal kingdom.

If the Temple is going to hold Glory, it cannot be built on platform. It must be built on government.

Platform Is Not Government

A platform amplifies a voice. Government carries responsibility for people. Confusing the two is one of the most damaging errors in modern church culture. Visibility is not authority, and influence is not government. A platform can grow quickly without structure; government cannot. When platform outpaces government, collapse is inevitable.

Scripture never equates being seen with being entrusted. In fact, Scripture repeatedly warns that visibility without stewardship leads to destruction. Authority is not measured by how many listen to you, but by how many you are responsible for before God. Crowds are impressed by gifting; heaven watches governance.

"Let a man so account of us, as of the ministers of Christ, and stewards of the mysteries of God." (1 Corinthians 4:1, KJV)

Platforms gather attention. Government carries weight. A platform can be sustained by charisma, but government requires character. This is why many leaders sound powerful but cannot sustain what they build. Their voice travels farther than their structure can support.

God does not entrust souls to voices; He entrusts souls to structures. Souls require oversight, correction, protection, and long-term care. A platform may inspire people, but it cannot shepherd them. Only government can do that.

This is why Scripture frames leadership not as celebrity, but as stewardship (1 Peter 5:2–3). Leaders are called to watch over souls, not rule over crowds. When a leader treats a platform as proof of authority, they begin to govern from affirmation rather than accountability. That is the beginning of collapse.

Platforms reward performance. Government demands restraint. Platforms grow through exposure; government grows through submission. The two obey different laws. When leaders try to govern by platform logic, they inevitably abuse authority, because platform logic is centered on self-preservation, while Kingdom government is centered on responsibility.

This distinction explains why God often allows platforms to grow while withholding authority. Visibility tests humility. Influence tests motive. Only when those tests are passed does God consider entrusting government. When leaders refuse that order, platform becomes a substitute for authority, and the house becomes vulnerable.

Many church failures do not occur because leaders lacked gifting, vision, or opportunity. They occur because leaders attempted to exercise government without first submitting to it.

They spoke with authority they had not yet earned, and they carried responsibility they had not yet learned to bear.

Authority that flows from platform is fragile. Authority that flows from stewardship is durable. God does not build His Kingdom on microphones; He builds it on faithful oversight.

Pastors Are Not Rulers - Christ Alone Is King

One of the most destructive distortions in modern church leadership is the quiet redefinition of pastors as rulers. This shift rarely happens openly. It happens subtly - through language, culture, expectation, and silence. Over time, shepherds become kings, oversight becomes control, and care is replaced by command. The Church absorbs Gentile authority models while still using biblical vocabulary to justify them.

Scripture does not support this distortion. Biblically, a ruler exercises sovereign authority, dominion, and ownership. Kings rule. Lords rule. Christ rules. Pastors were never given kingly authority over God's people. They were given responsibility for the flock, not dominion over it.

When pastors are treated as rulers, leadership shifts from Kingdom government to Gentile hierarchy. Authority becomes positional instead of functional. Obedience becomes enforced instead of discerned. Fear replaces trust, and silence is confused with unity. This model may produce order temporarily, but it always produces damage eventually.

Jesus addressed this directly - and forcefully.

"But Jesus called them unto him, and said, Ye know that the princes of the Gentiles exercise dominion over them, and they that are great exercise authority upon them. But it shall not be so among you." (Matthew 20:25–26, KJV)

That statement is not advice. It is a prohibition. Jesus did not soften it. He did not qualify it. He drew a clear line between Gentile authority systems and Kingdom government. The moment leadership crosses that line, it ceases to function as Kingdom authority, no matter how spiritual it sounds.

Pastors are called to watch over souls, not rule them (Hebrews 13:17). They are stewards, not sovereigns. When pastors assume kingly authority, they step outside their assignment and into a role God never authorized. That unauthorized authority must then be sustained by pressure rather than trust.

This principle is unmistakable in how authority functions in the Kingdom: control is always the substitute when true authority has not been earned. Ruling pastors rely on compliance because they lack the trust that produces willing alignment. They mistake silence for agreement and submission for spiritual maturity. But enforced obedience is not biblical submission - it is fear management.

Scripture provides a New Testament warning in Diotrephes, a leader who "loved to have the preeminence" and rejected apostolic correction (3 John 9–10). His issue was not doctrinal error; it was authority posture. He positioned himself as the gatekeeper of the house rather than a servant within it. Scripture does not commend him. It exposes him.

When pastors rule like kings, the house becomes unsafe. Correction is silenced. Discernment is punished. Loyalty is demanded rather than cultivated. Over time, truth leaves quietly, and dysfunction remains loudly defended.

Kingdom authority does not need to be enforced - it is recognized. It flows from trust, fruit, alignment, and proven care. Where those are absent, authority must be propped up with titles, threats, and spiritualized language. That is not strength; it is fragility.

Christ alone is King. Every other leader serves under His authority or not at all.

Hidden Places Test Trust

God always tests trust in obscurity before He restores it publicly. Hidden seasons are not delays; they are filters. They separate those who serve God from those who serve recognition. When visibility is removed, motives surface. When affirmation disappears, obedience is exposed for what it truly is.

Authority is never tested on a stage. It is tested in silence. It is tested when obedience carries no reward, when submission brings no recognition, and when faithfulness feels invisible. Many leaders desire restoration, but few are willing to remain faithful when no one is watching. God watches those seasons closely.

"And thy Father which seeth in secret himself shall reward thee openly." (Matthew 6:6, KJV)

Hidden places strip away performance. They remove the pressure to impress and expose the desire to be seen. In obscurity, leaders can no longer rely on gifting to carry them. They must rely on obedience. This is intentional. God does not want leaders who can perform publicly but collapse privately. He wants leaders whose inner life can sustain external responsibility.

David learned restraint in caves before he learned authority on a throne. In the cave, David had opportunity to seize power prematurely. He could have justified it spiritually. He could have framed it as destiny. Instead, he restrained himself. That restraint mattered more than his anointing. Authority returned to David because he proved he would not take what God had not yet released (1 Samual 24).

Hidden seasons also reveal how leaders respond to correction when there is no platform to validate them. Do they grow bitter, or do they grow sober? Do they withdraw in self-pity, or do they remain aligned? God uses obscurity to recalibrate a leader's relationship with authority itself.

One of the clearest indicators that trust is being rebuilt is contentment without position. When a leader no longer needs visibility to remain obedient, God knows authority will no longer be used to feed insecurity. Until that transformation occurs, restoration would be dangerous - not just for the leader, but for the people they would influence.

Obscurity is not punishment; it is protection. It shields the leader from premature exposure and shields the house from premature governance. Hidden faithfulness creates internal structure so that restored authority does not crush the carrier or fracture the community.

Those who despise hidden seasons often prove they are not ready for authority. Those who steward them faithfully reveal they are becoming safe.

Conclusion: The Test Is Government

Platform can be built fast. Government cannot.

A platform can gather people while a heart remains ungoverned. A platform can amplify gifting while trust is still fractured. But when pressure comes, what is ungoverned will always surface - because authority does not heal what obedience refused to crucify. It exposes it.

Saul proves the warning. When government collapses, discernment collapses. Promotion becomes perverse. Righteous men will not comply with unrighteous commands, so the leader finds a Doeg - someone willing to do what conscience will not permit. That is how houses get damaged: not only by what leaders do, but by what leaders empower.

This chapter is a line in the sand: platform is not government. Hidden places test trust. Correction tests humility. Restraint tests alignment. And God does not re-entrust weight where obedience is selective and accountability is negotiable.

If we want a house that can hold Glory, we cannot build it on popularity. We build it on government.

Scripture Index

- Matthew 6:6
- Matthew 15:14
- Matthew 20:25–26
- Hebrews 13:17 1
- Corinthians 3:9 1
- Corinthians 4:1 1
- Peter 5:2–3
- 1 Samuel 15:22–23
- 1 Samuel 21:1–9
- 1 Samuel 22:9–10
- 1 Samuel 22:17–18
- 1 Samuel 24
- 3 John 1:9–10

Chapter Eleven

Authority Re-Entrusted

Introduction: Weight Returns Where Alignment Remains

Authority can be lost quickly. But it is restored slowly.

Not because God is reluctant to forgive - He is rich in mercy. But because authority is not a feeling. It is government. And government cannot be rebuilt by emotion, time, or a public reset. Government is rebuilt by alignment - tested, proven, and sustained.

This chapter is about re-entrustment.

Not returning someone to a platform - returning someone to weight.

Because forgiveness restores relationship, but trust restores stewardship. And God does not re-release authority where the root remains unchanged. He re-entrusts weight where obedience is no longer selective, where correction is no longer resisted, where accountability is no longer negotiated, and where service - not status - has become the motive.

"The Son can do nothing of himself, but what he seeth the Father do…" (John 5:19, KJV)

That is the model of alignment. Authority remains where self-rule dies.

So this final part establishes the markers: what fruit signals restoration, why some are forgiven but never re-entrusted, and why Glory only rests on a house that can carry government. Because a Temple that will hold Glory must first hold authority - cleanly, humbly, and without private exceptions.

Authority Returns Where Alignment Remains

Authority does not return simply because time has passed or emotions have settled. Authority returns where alignment remains intact. Alignment is not agreement, preference, or personality compatibility. Alignment is order. It is the willingness to remain positioned correctly even when correction is uncomfortable and restraint feels costly.

Many leaders confuse alignment with silence. Silence is not alignment. Silence can be fear, exhaustion, or disengagement. Alignment is active. It is expressed through continued obedience, teachability, and submission to structure even when personal desires are delayed. Where alignment fractures, authority must remain withheld - not as rejection, but as protection.

"The Son can do nothing of himself, but what he seeth the Father do." (John 5:19, KJV)

Jesus modeled perfect alignment. Though fully anointed, He refused to act independently. His authority flowed directly from submission. This pattern exposes a common misconception in leadership culture - that authority increases with independence. In the Kingdom, authority increases with alignment.

Misalignment does not always look like rebellion. Often it looks like partial obedience, selective submission, or private resistance masked by public compliance. Leaders may appear aligned outwardly while quietly positioning themselves inwardly. God discerns that difference. Authority will not rest where alignment is performative rather than genuine.

Fractured alignment always fractures the house. When leaders operate independently while claiming submission, confusion spreads. People no longer know which voice carries weight. Authority becomes blurred, responsibility becomes diluted, and order erodes quietly. Voices compete. Responsibility fragments. God will not restore authority into an environment where alignment is claimed publicly but violated privately. God does not pour restored authority into confusion - He waits until order is repaired.

Alignment is tested most intensely when correction touches identity. When leaders must choose between preserving self-image and preserving order, the choice they make reveals readiness. Those who remain aligned under correction demonstrate that authority will not be used to protect ego. Those who resist correction reveal that authority would be used defensively.

This is why some leaders remain spiritually restored but structurally sidelined. God honors their repentance but withholds authority because alignment has not yet stabilized. Authority requires agreement with order, not merely agreement with outcome.

Where alignment remains, authority can return gradually and safely. Where alignment is fractured, restoration must pause. God does not rush authority into environments where it will multiply confusion rather than produce clarity.

Alignment is the channel through which authority flows. Break the channel, and authority leaks. Restore the channel, and authority can return.

Why Some Are Never Re-Entrusted with Authority

One of the most difficult truths for leaders to accept is that restoration of relationship does not obligate restoration of authority. Grace restores people. Authority governs houses. Scripture never confuses the two, even when modern leadership culture does.

Forgiveness is immediate when repentance is genuine. Re-entrustment is not. Authority carries consequences beyond the individual, and God will not gamble with the flock to validate someone's personal restoration. Love does not require position. Mercy does not demand government.

This distinction is not harsh - it is protective.

Scripture gives a sobering example in Eli and his sons. Eli was not condemned for ignorance; he was condemned for restraint withheld too long. His sons were corrupt, abusive, and unrestrained, and Eli knew it. God judged Eli not for what he did, but for what he allowed.

"For I have told him that I will judge his house for ever for the iniquity which he knoweth; because his sons made themselves vile, and he restrained them not." (1 Samuel 3:13, KJV)

God did not debate Eli's sincerity. He judged his stewardship. The failure was not relational; it was governmental. Eli may have loved his sons, but love did not excuse his refusal to protect the house. As a result, authority was removed - not only from his sons, but from his lineage.

This principle has not changed. Leaders may be forgiven, restored relationally, and even healed inwardly - yet still remain unqualified for authority. Not because God is withholding grace, but because authority affects others. God's responsibility is not only to the leader; it is to the people entrusted to that leader's care.

This is why Scripture repeatedly separates spiritual maturity from positional authority. Desire does not qualify. Tears do not qualify. Time alone does not qualify. Only proven change over time qualifies, and even then, restoration of authority is not guaranteed.

Some leaders confuse sidelining with rejection. Scripture does not. Being removed from authority is often an act of mercy.

It prevents further damage, allows healing to occur without pressure, and protects the house from repeated instability. Authority is not a right - it is a trust.

"Obey them that have the rule over you, and submit yourselves: for they watch for your souls." (Hebrews 13:17, KJV)

That verse explains why God is cautious. Leaders are accountable for souls. When authority is mishandled, people suffer quietly and long after the leader has moved on. God does not restore authority simply because a leader is eager to return. He restores authority when it is safe for others.

There are leaders God loves deeply who will never lead again in the same way. That is not abandonment. It is wisdom. The Kingdom does not require every restored person to be re-positioned. It requires the house to be protected.

Authority withheld is not always judgment. Sometimes it is stewardship.

Illustration - When a House Is Not Yet Healed

There was a church that experienced the departure of a long-standing pastor. The separation was necessary, but the house had not yet processed the weight of the transition. Leadership believed enough time had passed and invited a guest speaker to minister. On the surface, the decision appeared harmless.

But the guest looked like the former pastor. He sounded like him. He carried the same cadence, mannerisms, and presence.

Almost immediately, the atmosphere shifted. Old emotions surfaced. Familiar attachments were triggered. The room responded not to the message, but to the memory.

The leadership had to intervene and ask the guest not to speak.

Nothing doctrinal was wrong. Nothing immoral occurred. But the house reacted because the wound had not yet closed, and authority had not yet been re-stabilized. The issue was not the guest - it was timing. The house was not ready to carry that weight again.

This is exactly why God withholds authority even when intentions are sincere. Restoration is not about readiness to speak; it is about readiness to govern. A house can forgive before it can trust. It can heal relationally before it is stable structurally.

When authority is reintroduced too early - even indirectly - it can reopen what God is still closing. God does not rush this process, because souls are involved. What leadership may see as progress, God may see as premature exposure.

This is why some leaders are loved but not re-positioned. Not because God is withholding grace, but because the house has not yet regained its equilibrium. Authority returned too soon does not strengthen a house - it destabilizes it.

The Fruit That Signals Restoration

God does not announce restoration; He observes it. Long before authority is returned publicly, fruit begins to appear privately. Scripture never points to intention as evidence - only fruit. Desire can be sincere and still dangerous. Words can be correct and still premature. God watches what remains when pressure is applied and recognition is withheld.

Fruit is not momentary behavior; it is sustained pattern. It appears slowly, consistently, and without demand for validation. Restored leaders do not argue for position. They do not campaign for visibility. They do not interpret patience as rejection. Instead, they demonstrate restraint, sobriety, teachability, and endurance over time.

"Wherefore by their fruits ye shall know them." (Matthew 7:20, KJV)

One of the clearest signs that trust is being rebuilt is self-governance. Leaders who have been restored inwardly but not yet re-entrusted outwardly no longer push against boundaries. They honor limits instead of resenting them. They value order more than opportunity. They demonstrate that authority, when returned, will be carried rather than consumed.

Another marker of restored trust is how a leader responds when their voice is not centered. Do they remain aligned when overlooked? Do they remain faithful when not consulted? Do they support decisions they did not influence? These moments reveal far more than public ministry ever could.

Fruit also shows up in how leaders handle correction after restoration. Corrected leaders who have truly changed no longer defend themselves reflexively. They listen. They weigh counsel. They adjust without posture. They no longer interpret correction as threat, because authority is no longer feeding identity.

Time is essential in this process. Scripture consistently places distance between repentance and promotion. Not because God is slow, but because fruit takes time to mature. Quick restoration often masks unresolved patterns. Slow restoration reveals whether transformation is real.

This is why God often allows fruit to speak quietly before authority speaks publicly. When fruit is undeniable, authority becomes safe. When fruit is absent, authority would be reckless.

Authority Is Returned for Service, Not Status

When authority is finally restored, it feels different than before. It is heavier. Quieter. Less exciting. The thrill of position has been replaced by the weight of responsibility. Leaders who are ready for restored authority no longer seek status - they accept obligation.

"Whosoever will be great among you, let him be your minister." (Matthew 20:26, KJV)

Authority returned for status seeks recognition. Authority returned for service seeks protection of the house. One builds platforms; the other builds people. God restores authority only when ambition has been stripped away and service has become the priority.

This is why restored authority often looks smaller than expected. God is not interested in spectacle; He is interested in sustainability. He entrusts authority to those who will use it to strengthen others, not themselves.

A House That Can Carry Authority Can Carry Glory

Glory does not rest on gifting. It rests on order. Scripture consistently connects God's presence to righteous governance. Where authority is handled correctly, heaven remains. Where authority is abused, heaven withdraws - not in anger, but in restraint.

"And the key of the house of David will I lay upon his shoulder." (Isaiah 22:22, KJV)

Keys represent responsibility, not privilege. Shoulders carry weight, not applause. When authority is carried correctly, God is comfortable remaining. When authority is mishandled, God removes weight before damage multiplies.

This is why trust must be rebuilt before authority is restored. Glory is too valuable to be placed in unstable hands.

Houses that honor order can carry presence. Houses that confuse authority with entitlement cannot.

Conclusion: Weight Returns Where Obedience Remains

Authority does not return because desire returned. It returns when a house has become safe enough to carry weight again.

God re-entrusts weight where alignment remains - where obedience is no longer selective, where correction is received without revolt, where accountability is honored without manipulation, and where the motive is service, not status. Forgiveness restores relationship, but trust restores stewardship. And trust is rebuilt through fruit, not through claims.

This is why some are restored relationally but never re-entrusted with government: patterns stayed alive. The root remained. The vessel could not carry weight without repeating the fracture. But where repentance produces measurable change - where restraint is embraced, where humility is visible, where stability returns - authority can be safely returned.

And here is the final measure: the Glory of God does not rest on hype. It rests on order. A house that can carry authority can carry Glory - because government holds what presence exposes.

So the call is simple and severe:

Stay aligned. Stay submitted. Serve without needing preeminence.

Because in the Kingdom, weight returns where obedience remains.

Scripture Index

- Proverbs 29:1
- Matthew 7:20
- Matthew 20:26–27
- Luke 16:10
- John 5:19
- Hebrews 13:17
- 1 Peter 4:17
- Isaiah 22:22
- 1 Samuel 3:13

Chapter Twelve

The River Is Not Withheld, It Is Weighed

Introduction: The River Carries Weight, Not Emotion

The River of God is not an emotional current. It is not a spiritual experience designed to make people feel alive. It is not an atmosphere, a mood, momentum, or the byproduct of worship.

The River carries weight.

Throughout Scripture, the River is never separated from government, order, life, and authority. Wherever the River flows, something is ruled, something is healed, something is judged, or something is brought into alignment. The River does not drift. It does not wander. It does not adapt to disorder. It flows with purpose and consequence. It is never passive. It never flows without effect. It never touches without consequence.

That is why the River cannot be separated from authority. And it cannot be understood through experience alone. Experience responds to sensation. The River responds to structure.

From Eden to Ezekiel, from the Temple to the New Jerusalem, the River is never introduced as optional. It is released to establish the rule of God in the earth.

Authority is not permission; it is weight. Weight tests structure. Weight exposes weakness. Weight reveals whether something can stand under pressure. It reveals whether a house, a leader, or a vessel can stand without fracturing.

The River operates the same way.

God does not release the River to entertain or excite a house. He releases the River to govern it.

If a house cannot carry authority, it cannot carry the River. If a vessel leaks obedience, it will leak life. If alignment fractures, flow is restricted.

And let this boundary be clear: this obedience is first and foremost to God and His Word - not to a man in a suit calling himself a pastor. Scripture never assigns ultimate authority to titles. It assigns authority to obedience, faithfulness, and alignment with God's rule.

Much confusion has entered the Church through the misinterpretation of passages such as *"obey them that have the rule over you"* (Hebrews 13:17, KJV).

Hebrews 13:17 (KJV) *"Obey them that have the rule over you, and submit yourselves: for they watch for your souls, as they that must give account..."*

The word translated *obey* (*peithō*) does not mean blind compliance. It means to be persuaded, to trust, to yield because one is convinced. This is relational and conditional, not authoritarian.

You obey because the leader is aligned with Christ and Scripture, not because of a title.

Obedience flows from alignment with Christ and the Word - not from position, rank, or religious office.

Authority Is Limited to Scripture

Church leadership authority exists only where Scripture exists.

A leader is not authorized to rule your life by preference, personality, control, or private opinions. The moment authority detaches from Scripture, it becomes something else entirely: domination, manipulation, or spiritual intimidation.

"We ought to obey God rather than men." (Acts 5:29, KJV)

That command was never revoked. Hebrews 13:17 does not cancel it. It assumes a leader is operating under God's government - because the Church is not built on personal kingdoms. It is built on Christ's rule.

So here is the boundary in plain terms:

If a leader tells you not to sin - submit. If a leader calls you to repentance - submit. If a leader urges you toward forgiveness, holiness, truth, reconciliation, maturity, and obedience - submit. If a leader instructs you to violate Scripture, hide sin, excuse sin, or participate in sin - refuse. If a leader uses position to demand loyalty against truth - refuse. If a leader requires silence where God requires light - refuse.

"For there is nothing covered, that shall not be revealed; neither hid, that shall not be known." (Luke 12:2, KJV)

Authority that demands secrecy to survive is not Kingdom authority. The Kingdom operates in light. God's government can withstand examination.

"And have no fellowship with the unfruitful works of darkness, but rather reprove them." (Ephesians 5:11, KJV)

So biblical submission is not blind compliance - it is alignment with God's Word. You submit to leaders as they lead under Scripture, not as they drift into control.

If Scripture is the boundary, then Scripture is also the protection.

That is why the Church fractures when leaders treat authority like ownership. They forget they are stewards. They forget they must give account. They forget the people belong to Christ, not to them.

"Neither as being lords over God's heritage, but being ensamples to the flock." (1 Peter 5:3, KJV)

When authority stays inside Scripture, it produces protection and maturity. When it steps outside Scripture, it produces fear and bondage. One is Kingdom government. The other is Babylon.

The Veil Was Torn: No Human Gatekeepers

When Jesus died, the veil in the temple was torn from top to bottom.

"And, behold, the veil of the temple was rent in twain from the top to the bottom…" (Matthew 27:51, KJV) *"And the veil of the temple was rent in twain from the top to the bottom."* (Mark 15:38, KJV) *"And the sun was darkened, and the veil of the temple was rent in the midst."* (Luke 23:45, KJV)

Top to bottom means God did it. Not man. That tear was a verdict: the era of priestly gatekeeping was finished. No more curtains. No more controlled access. No more "you can only come through us."

And this is not where the problem started. The problem started at the mountain.

God invited a nation to come near, but they refused intimacy and demanded distance.

"Speak thou with us, and we will hear: but let not God speak with us, lest we die." (Exodus 20:19, KJV) *"Go thou near, and hear all that the LORD our God shall say… and we will hear it, and do it."* (Deuteronomy 5:27, KJV)

That refusal birthed a religious mindset: "Let someone else deal with God. Just manage us."

And fallen men will always try to turn that arrangement into control.

So God did what religion hates: He removed priestly mediation as a control point by placing priesthood and access into Christ Himself.

"Seeing then that we have a great high priest... let us therefore come boldly..." (Hebrews 4:14–16, KJV) *"Having therefore, brethren, boldness to enter into the holiest by the blood of Jesus..."* (Hebrews 10:19–22, KJV) *"For there is one God, and one mediator between God and men, the man Christ Jesus."* (1 Timothy 2:5, KJV)

That means church leaders are not mediators. They are not gatekeepers of your access to God. They serve under the King. They teach, guard, and watch - but they do not replace the voice of Christ, and they do not own the people.

And Jesus confronted religious leaders who used religion to dominate. He didn't flatter them. He named them.

"Ye serpents, ye generation of vipers..." (Matthew 23:33, KJV)

He said that because religious control is not harmless - it destroys relationship. It replaces love with fear. It replaces truth with image-management. It replaces repentance with performance.

And remember this: leaders deal with sin like everyone else.

"If we say that we have no sin, we deceive ourselves..." (1 John 1:8, KJV)

Yes - leaders should meet biblical standards of character and self-control (1 Timothy 3:1–7; Titus 1:7–9). But they can still fail. Some are fighting to keep it hidden. Some are battling things worse than what you're battling. That is exactly why your faith cannot be built on a man's stability. It must be built on Christ's government.

God's desire was never a population managed by intermediaries. His desire was a people who know Him - a kingdom of priests.

"And ye shall be unto me a kingdom of priests..." (Exodus 19:6, KJV) *"But ye are a chosen generation, a royal priesthood..."* (1 Peter 2:9, KJV) *"They shall all know me, from the least to the greatest..."* (Jeremiah 31:34, KJV; Hebrews 8:11, KJV)

So yes - God created the Church so He could deal with your issues directly: by His Spirit, through His Word, in the light - while leaders function as watchers and servants, not masters and gatekeepers.

They Watch for Your Souls - What Hebrews 13:17 Actually Means

Hebrews 13:17 is one of the most abused verses in modern church culture - not because the verse is unclear, but because people read it like Babylon reads authority.

"Obey them that have the rule over you, and submit yourselves: for they watch for your souls, as they that must give account..." (Hebrews 13:17)

That verse is not a blank check for control.

It does not create a priesthood of gatekeepers. The veil was torn (Matthew 27:51). Christ is the only mediator (1 Timothy 2:5). Access is open (Hebrews 10:19–22). So whatever Hebrews 13:17

means, it cannot mean "submit to a man as though he is your doorway to God."

The verse gives a boundary inside the verse itself:

"for they watch for your souls, as they that must give account" (Hebrews 13:17, KJV).

That means their authority is defined by their assignment: watching - guarding, warning, teaching, correcting, and protecting people from deception, sin, and destruction. It is spiritual oversight, not personal ownership.

And they are accountable for it.

They *"must give account"* (Hebrews 13:17, KJV). Account to whom? Not the crowd. Not the denomination. Not social media. They answer to God.

So Hebrews 13:17 is not saying, "leaders are always right." It is saying, "leaders carry responsibility, and God will judge them for how they watch."

That immediately limits what you are being asked to submit to.

Submission in the Kingdom is never submission to manipulation. It is submission to biblical correction, biblical warning, biblical teaching, biblical protection, and biblical order.

You are not called to bow to secrecy that exists to protect image. You are not called to yield to intimidation designed to silence truth. You are not called to honor preferences that have been lifted above Scripture. And you are not called to submit to control that replaces relationship with fear.

Because the Kingdom operates in light.

"For there is nothing covered, that shall not be revealed; neither hid, that shall not be known." (Luke 12:2, KJV)

And Scripture gives the posture leaders must carry:

"Feed the flock of God... not as being lords over God's heritage, but being ensamples to the flock." (1 Peter 5:2–3, KJV)

So Hebrews 13:17 cannot be used to build kings. It is written to produce shepherds - men who serve, protect, and watch without domination.

And here is another boundary that matters: leaders deal with sin like everyone else.

"If we say that we have no sin, we deceive ourselves..." (1 John 1:8, KJV)

That is why your submission must never be blind. It must be biblical. Leaders are called to meet standards (1 Timothy 3:1–7; Titus 1:7–9), but they are still men. Some fail quietly. Some fail loudly. Some hide. Some repent. Some don't.

So biblical submission is not: "I follow no matter what." Biblical submission is: "I follow you as you follow Christ."

And that is exactly why Hebrews 13:17 is paired with accountability: the leader watches, the leader answers to God, and the people are protected by Scripture - not trapped by control.

Pastoral Authority Is a Demotion, Not a Promotion

Pastoral authority is not a promotion into status. It is a demotion into service.

If a man thinks leadership makes him higher, he already does not understand the Kingdom. In the Kingdom, leadership does not lift you above the flock - it puts you under responsibility for the flock. It does not grant privilege. It assigns burden.

That is why Scripture does not describe pastors as kings. It describes them as shepherds, servants, and stewards - men who will give account to God for how they handled people's souls. (Hebrews 13:17)

Jesus is the model and the boundary.

"Ye know that the princes of the Gentiles exercise dominion over them... But it shall not be so among you..." (Matthew 20:25–26, KJV)

"Not so among you" is not a suggestion. It is a prohibition. The moment a leader crosses into dominion, he has stepped into the spirit of the Gentiles, not the government of Christ.

Kingdom authority moves downward.

"And whosoever will be chief among you, let him be your servant." (Matthew 20:27, KJV)

That is demotion language.

It means the closer you get to real authority, the more you are required to serve. The more weight you carry, the less you get to live for yourself. The more responsibility you receive, the less you get to "do what you want."

A true pastor is not crowned. A true pastor is assigned. And the assignment is costly.

"Feed the flock of God… taking the oversight thereof… not as being lords over God's heritage, but being ensamples to the flock." (1 Peter 5:2–3, KJV)

Oversight is not ownership. Oversight is accountability. Oversight is watching, guarding, warning, correcting, and protecting - while living as an example.

That is why pastoral authority is a demotion: you are demoted from self-interest. Demoted from ego. Demoted from private life. Demoted from being "just one of the people." Because now your decisions touch other people's stability.

And this is where many leaders fail: they want the authority without the demotion.

They want to be heard, but not questioned. They want to correct others, but not be corrected. They want honor, but not accountability. They want platform, but not scrutiny.

But Hebrews 13:17 will not allow that. It declares that leaders *"must give account."* (Hebrews 13:17, KJV)

That means leadership is not a throne - it is a courtroom. One day, God will ask what you did with the people He entrusted to you.

So if a man is craving the title, he is not ready for the weight.

Because in the Kingdom, leadership is not upward mobility. It is downward responsibility. It is not promotion. It is demotion - into the posture of Christ.

"The Son of man came not to be ministered unto, but to minister..." (Mark 10:45, KJV)

And that is the standard. Not charisma. Not control. Not religious dominance. Christlike service under government.

The River Is Not Withheld - It Is Weighed

The River of God is not scarce.

It is selective.

God is not reluctant to release life. He is careful where He releases it. The River carries authority, judgment, healing, exposure, and establishment. It does not flow safely through unstable structures. It does not rest in houses that reject government. It does not strengthen leaders who refuse demotion.

The River is not withheld because God is stingy. It is weighed because God is holy.

In Ezekiel's vision, the River does not begin in the street. It begins at the Temple.

"Afterward he brought me again unto the door of the house; and, behold, waters issued out from under the threshold of the house..." (Ezekiel 47:1, KJV)

The flow proceeds outward from the place of order. It increases gradually - ankles, knees, loins - until it becomes waters to swim in (Ezekiel 47:3–5). That progression is not accidental. The River deepens where structure can sustain it.

If the Temple is fractured, the River exposes it. If leadership is unstable, the River magnifies it. If authority is ungoverned, the River does not bless - it destabilizes.

That is why judgment begins at the house of God.

"For the time is come that judgment must begin at the house of God..." (1 Peter 4:17, KJV)

Judgment does not mean destruction first. It means evaluation. It means weighing. It means exposure. God measures alignment before He releases increase.

When the River came in Acts 2, it did not produce chaos. It produced order, repentance, and submission to apostolic doctrine.

"And they continued stedfastly in the apostles' doctrine and fellowship..." (Acts 2:42, KJV)

The River did not eliminate authority. It strengthened it. It did not remove government. It clarified it.

But when leadership refuses demotion - when it clings to dominance, hides sin, resists accountability - the River does not empower that structure. It confronts it.

Because the River is not emotional movement. It is divine government in motion.

And here is the sobering truth: many houses ask for revival while resisting order. They ask for Glory while refusing correction.

They want flow without submission. But the River flows where government can remain.

If authority cannot stay aligned, the River cannot stay flowing.

That is why God weighs leaders. He measures obedience. He tests humility. He exposes hidden pride before He releases greater depth.

The River is not withheld. It is weighed.

Conclusion: The River Flows Where Government Can Remain

God is not reluctant to release the River. He is careful where He releases it.

The River carries authority, life, judgment, healing, and government. It cannot be entrusted to structures that leak obedience or vessels that resist submission. It will not empower domination. It will not strengthen priestly gatekeeping. The veil was torn (Matthew 27:51). Access is in Christ (Hebrews 10:19–22). Leadership is stewardship under accountability, not control.

That is why pastoral authority is a demotion. The River does not flow through thrones built by ego. It flows through servants who can carry weight without demanding status - men who watch for souls and will give account (Hebrews 13:17). Where leaders live under government, the house stabilizes. Where the house stabilizes, the River deepens.

And if judgment begins at the house of God (1 Peter 4:17), then the first thing God weighs is not the crowd - it is the government of the house. Not the noise. Not the numbers. The obedience. The alignment. The humility.

The River is not coming. The River is already flowing.

The question is not whether heaven is willing. The question is whether the house is aligned.

Scripture Index

- Acts 2:42
- Ezekiel 47:1–5
- Hebrews 10:19–22
- Hebrews 13:17
- 1 Peter 4:17
- Matthew 20:25–27
- Mark 10:45
- Matthew 27:51
- 1 Timothy 2:5
- Luke 12:2
- 1 Peter 5:2–3
- Exodus 20:19
- Deuteronomy 5:27
- Hebrews 4:14–16
- Matthew 23:33
- 1 John 1:8
- 1 Timothy 3:1–7
- Titus 1:7–9

Chapter Thirteen

Equip the Saint

Introduction: The Goal Was Never Attendance

The goal of the Church was never attendance. It was never crowd size. It was never activity. It was never enthusiasm.

The goal was equipment.

"And he gave some, apostles; and some, prophets; and some, evangelists; and some, pastors and teachers; For the perfecting of the saints, for the work of the ministry, for the edifying of the body of Christ." (Ephesians 4:11–12, KJV)

From the beginning, God did not design a system where a few perform and the many observe. He designed a body - where every member functions, carries responsibility, and bears weight. The moment the Church shifted from equipping saints to entertaining believers, authority began to leak and glory began to thin.

A saint is not someone who sits. A saint is someone who is prepared.

The Church does not exist to replace personal responsibility with professional religion. It exists to restore sons and daughters to function, to return people to alignment with the Kingdom, and to train them to carry what heaven releases.

If the River flows but the saints are not equipped, the River will be wasted. If glory appears but the saints are not trained, collapse will follow.

God does not pour weight into unprepared vessels.

What "Equip" Actually Means - The Word *Fit*

"And he gave some, apostles; and some, prophets; and some, evangelists; and some, pastors and teachers; For the perfecting of the saints, for the work of the ministry, for the edifying of the body of Christ." (Ephesians 4:11–12, KJV)

The word translated *"perfecting"* in Ephesians 4:12 (KJV) is the Greek word *katartismos*. It does not mean flawlessness. It does not mean spiritual celebrity. It means to be made fit, restored to proper condition, set in order, or brought into alignment for function.

It carries the idea of something that was out of joint being put back into place.

That is the same root idea used when James and John were "mending" their nets.

"And going on from thence, he saw other two brethren… mending their nets…" (Matthew 4:21, KJV)

The nets were not being decorated. They were being repaired so they could function.

That is equipping.

Equipping is not applause. It is repair. It is strengthening what is weak, straightening what is crooked, training what is immature, stabilizing what is unstable, and restoring to working condition what has been broken.

It is not inspiration - it is alignment.

Paul's language makes the structure clear:

"For the perfecting (katartismos) of the saints, for the work of the ministry, for the edifying of the body of Christ." (Ephesians 4:12, KJV)

Saints are made fit so they can work. They are restored so they can carry weight. They are aligned so the body can be built.

And that means something uncomfortable: equipping requires adjustment.

When a bone is out of joint, resetting it hurts. When a net is torn, repairing it takes tension. When a saint is immature, training exposes weakness.

That is why equipping cannot be confused with entertaining. Entertainment leaves people comfortable. Equipping leaves people functional.

The Church was never commissioned to create spectators. It was commissioned to produce saints who are fit for ministry - stable enough to carry authority, mature enough to resist deception, disciplined enough to obey under pressure.

If the saints are not fit, the body cannot be built. If the body is not built, the River cannot deepen. If the River cannot deepen, glory cannot remain.

Equipping is not optional. It is the structure that allows the house to stand.

Why the Church Became Dependent

Dependence is not a neutral condition in the Kingdom.

When the saints are not equipped, they do not become harmless - they become dependent. And dependence always produces the same outcomes: fragility, immaturity, and control structures.

A dependent church is a church where people cannot discern without a personality. They cannot obey without being pushed. They cannot endure correction without leaving. They cannot handle offense without collapsing. They cannot carry responsibility without blaming leadership.

That is not strength. That is infancy.

Paul did not describe the Church as a crowd gathered around a professional speaker. He described the Church as a body - every joint, every member, every part supplying what is needed.

"From whom the whole body fitly joined together and compacted by that which every joint supplieth... maketh increase of the body..." (Ephesians 4:16, KJV)

The body increases when joints supply. The body does not increase when one organ performs while the rest remain idle.

So how does a house drift into dependence, then treat that as normal?

Leaders Drifted from Equipping into Performing

Equipping is slower than performing. Equipping requires patience. It requires correction. It requires building people until they can function without you. Performance requires none of that. It can gather a crowd, create excitement, and still leave the saints unchanged.

But God did not give gifts to replace the saints. He gave gifts to prepare them.

"And he gave some… pastors and teachers; For the perfecting of the saints…" (Ephesians 4:11–12, KJV)

If leadership is doing all the work, the saints are not equipped. And if the saints are not equipped, the Church becomes a stage, not a body.

People Learned to Prefer Comfort over Growth

Equipping confronts the flesh. It exposes immaturity. It presses responsibility onto the believer. It removes excuses. It trains obedience. Many people resist that process because it demands change.

"For the time will come when they will not endure sound doctrine…" (2 Timothy 4:3, KJV)

When people will not endure doctrine, they seek what is easy, entertaining, and affirming. And where that hunger exists, leaders can be tempted to feed it instead of cure it.

Dependence Creates a Control Economy

Where saints are not equipped, leaders become necessary for everything. When leaders become necessary for everything, control becomes easy.

Not always intentional. Sometimes it's just the result of neglect. But the outcome is the same: the people stop functioning and start orbiting.

That is why some churches panic when people mature. Mature saints ask questions. Mature saints discern. Mature saints require Scripture. Mature saints do not submit to manipulation. Mature saints can obey God without needing a personality to approve it.

And if a system survives on dependence, maturity becomes a threat.

The Saints Were Never Trained to Hear the King

A dependent church often produces believers who know sermons but do not know the Shepherd.

"My sheep hear my voice… and they follow me." (John 10:27, KJV)

Equipping trains the saint to recognize the voice of Christ in Scripture, to obey without constant handholding, and to stand without emotional reinforcement. When saints are not trained to hear the King, they become vulnerable to deception, trends, and charismatic domination.

That is why equipping is not optional. It is protection.

The goal is not a house full of people who need you. The goal is a body full of saints who can carry weight.

Many Saints Leave Their Helmet at Church

A great tragedy in the modern church is that many people have learned how to look spiritual in a service, but they were never equipped to stand in a battle. They know how to say amen. They know how to shout hallelujah. They know how to lift their hands at the right moment and sound alive in the room. But noise is not armor, performance is not strength, and activity is not maturity.

It became a cultural spectacle in the 1970s and 1980s for people to run across football fields and baseball stadiums buck naked, screaming for attention. It was foolish, shameful, exposed, and humiliating. And the church has produced its own version of that spectacle in the spirit.

Too many believers have the helmet of salvation on and nothing else. They are spiritual streakers in the house of God.

And many do not even keep that helmet on. They leave the helmet of salvation at church and live the rest of their lives without it. They know how to look saved in the room, but they do not know how to live covered when the room is gone.

Some of the worst cases are ministers, so-called armor bearers, and teachers. They know how to move in church culture and appear spiritual in public, but when people are not looking, the fruit changes. Love is missing. Peace is missing. Meekness is missing. Temperance is missing. And when the fruit of the Spirit is missing, position cannot hide exposure (Galatians 5:22–23).

Scripture never taught that salvation was the whole armor. It taught that salvation was one piece of it. *"Take the helmet of salvation, and the sword of the Spirit, which is the word of God"* (Ephesians 6:17, KJV). And again, *"Put on the whole armour of God, that ye may be able to stand against the wiles of the devil"* (Ephesians 6:11, KJV).

You are not immune to sin. You are not immune to demons. You are not immune to sickness. You are not immune to a body that decays and dies. That is why you need armor. If you were immune, God would not have told you to dress for war. The armor is proof the battle is real and the danger is real.

This is where false church language has to be judged. "Armor bearer" may be biblical as a military role in Israel's history, but it is not a New Testament church office. Saul had one. Jonathan had one (1 Samuel 14:6–7; 1 Samuel 16:21). But Christ did not establish armor bearers in His house. He gave apostles, prophets, evangelists, pastors, and teachers for equipping the saints, along with elders and deacons for order and oversight (Ephesians 4:11–12; 1 Timothy 3:1–13; Titus 1:5–9).

And the reason is plain: you are supposed to be wearing the armor, not handing it to another person to carry for you. *"Put on the whole armour of God"* (Ephesians 6:11, KJV). That command was given to the believer, not to an assistant standing beside him. In the kingdom, you do not remove your helmet so someone else can mind it. You do not hand off your shield so someone else can maintain it. You do not outsource your covering. Spiritual armor is meant to stay on the saint. So the issue is not who is close to a leader. The issue is who is actually clothed before God.

This is where the weakness of an unequipped church becomes obvious. People perform spirituality in public while remaining uncovered in character. Envy still rules them. Control still rules them. Compromise still rules them. Lying, gossip, lust, and fleshly appetite still leak through their life. Then they act as if proximity to ministry made them immune. It did not.

A believer is not called to act armed. A believer is called to be armed.

That is why equipping is not optional. If saints are not trained in truth, discipline, obedience, fruit, and spiritual maturity, they remain vulnerable. They become loud, but not stable. Visible, but not weight-bearing. Present, but not prepared. And a church full of people like that cannot carry glory for long, because what is uncovered will eventually be struck.

The goal of leadership is not to gather crowds who know how to respond in a service. The goal is to form saints who can stand in truth, hear the King, resist compromise, bear the fruit of the Spirit, and remain covered when the room gets quiet. Saints must not only be inspired. They must be dressed for war.

The Work of the Ministry Belongs to the Saints

The work of the ministry was never designed to be performed by a few professionals while the many watch.

It belongs to the saints.

Ephesians does not whisper it. It declares it:

"For the perfecting of the saints, for the work of the ministry, for the edifying of the body of Christ." (Ephesians 4:12, KJV)

The order is violent if you take it seriously:

Saints are made fit.

Saints do the work.

The body is built.

So when "ministry" becomes something only the platform does, the entire structure is inverted. The gifts of leadership begin replacing the saints instead of equipping them. The body becomes dependent. The joints stop supplying. Growth becomes cosmetic instead of structural.

This is why many churches can grow in attendance and still shrink in maturity.

Because the metric is wrong.

Saints are not spectators

The New Testament pattern is not clergy and audience. It is body and function. Every believer is called to bear fruit. Every believer is called to carry responsibility. Every believer is called to obey, endure, forgive, resist temptation, walk in holiness, and serve.

"I beseech you therefore, brethren… that ye present your bodies a living sacrifice…" (Romans 12:1, KJV)

That is not written to leaders only. That is written to the Church.

The saints build the house

A house is strengthened when many hands carry weight. A house is weakened when one man carries everything. This is why God gives gifts - not to monopolize ministry, but to multiply it.

"And he gave some… pastors and teachers…" (Ephesians 4:11, KJV)

These gifts are not replacements. They are trainers. Their job is to teach, correct, stabilize, and restore saints until saints can function.

A saint who is equipped becomes dangerous to darkness.

An equipped saint discerns lies. An equipped saint refuses temptation. An equipped saint confronts sin with truth. An equipped saint serves without needing credit. An equipped saint carries authority without needing a title. An equipped saint endures hardship without collapsing. An equipped saint builds others instead of consuming others.

That is what "fit" means. A net repaired. A bone set. A vessel able to carry weight.

So the question is not: "Do we have a good church service?" The question is: "Are the saints being equipped to do the work?"

Because if the saints are not working, the body is not building. And if the body is not building, the house cannot carry Glory.

Edifying the Body - Growth Is Structural

Edification is not emotional uplift.

It is structural strengthening.

Paul does not describe the Church as something that is merely inspired. He describes it as something that is **built**.

"For the perfecting of the saints, for the work of the ministry, for the edifying of the body of Christ." (Ephesians 4:12, KJV)

The word *edifying* means to build up, to construct, to strengthen from the inside out. It is architectural language. It assumes process. It assumes alignment. It assumes structure that can carry additional weight.

That means real growth is not measured by attendance spikes or emotional moments. It is measured by whether the body can endure pressure without fracturing.

Structural growth produces stability

Paul continues:

"Till we all come in the unity of the faith, and of the knowledge of the Son of God, unto a perfect man, unto the measure of the stature of the fulness of Christ." (Ephesians 4:13, KJV)

Unity of faith. Knowledge of the Son. Maturity. Measure. Fullness.

Those are structural words. They describe formation, not excitement.

And he explains why this structure matters:

"That we henceforth be no more children, tossed to and fro, and carried about with every wind of doctrine…" (Ephesians 4:14, KJV)

Children are unstable. Children react emotionally. Children follow trends. Children shift with pressure. But a body that has been edified does not drift with every teaching, personality, or movement.

So equipping protects against deception.

Growth is proven under pressure

If a church cannot endure correction, it is not built. If a church collapses when a leader fails, it was not built. If a church fractures when doctrine is challenged, it was not built.

Structural growth does not produce fragile people. It produces saints who discern, endure, forgive, confront sin without panic, and stay aligned when emotions fluctuate.

Paul gives the final mark of structural growth:

"But speaking the truth in love, may grow up into him in all things, which is the head, even Christ." (Ephesians 4:15, KJV)

Truth and love together create healthy structure. Truth without love hardens. Love without truth weakens. Together they build.

And Christ remains the Head.

That matters. Because when Christ is the Head, leaders are not. Saints are not dependent on personality. They are connected to the Head. That connection produces supply.

"From whom the whole body fitly joined together and compacted by that which every joint supplieth…" (Ephesians 4:16, KJV)

The body grows when joints supply. Growth is not driven by spotlight. It is driven by alignment and participation.

If the joints do not supply, the body cannot increase. If saints are not equipped, the structure weakens. If the structure weakens, the River cannot deepen.

Growth is not noise. Growth is structure.

Conclusion: The Church Was Built to Multiply Saints, Not Dependence

God did not build the Church to create a population that needs constant management. He built the Church to produce saints who are fit, functioning, and mature - so the body can carry weight without collapsing.

"For the perfecting of the saints, for the work of the ministry, for the edifying of the body of Christ." (Ephesians 4:12, KJV)

That is the blueprint.

Equipping is not inspiration. It is restoration and alignment. Ministry is not a stage. It is the saints doing the work. Growth is not hype. It is the body being built into stability.

And the target is not vague. The target is Christ:

"…unto the measure of the stature of the fulness of Christ." (Ephesians 4:13, KJV)

Until saints are equipped, the Church remains fragile - tossed by doctrine, ruled by emotion, dependent on personality. But when saints are equipped, the house becomes stable. When the house becomes stable, the River can deepen. When the River deepens, glory can remain.

So the question is not whether the service was good. The question is whether the saints are becoming fit.

Because the Kingdom does not advance through spectators. It advances through equipped saints who carry responsibility under Christ's Headship.

Scripture Index

- Ephesians 4:11–16
- Matthew 4:21
- 2 Timothy 4:3
- John 10:27
- Romans 12:1

Chapter Fourteen

When Identity Is Rebuilt

Introduction: Identity Is Rebuilt, Not Announced

Identity in the Kingdom is not a slogan you repeat. It is a structure God rebuilds.

Many people try to replace shame with a confession, but they never replace the foundation that produced the shame. They want freedom without formation. They want a new name without a new nature. They want to feel clean while still thinking like Babylon.

That is why the gospel does not merely forgive you - it recreates you.

"Therefore if any man be in Christ, he is a new creature: old things are passed away; behold, all things are become new." (2 Corinthians 5:17, KJV)

But new creature does not mean your mind is instantly trained. It means God placed something new inside you that must be governed until your life matches what heaven declared. The old identity does not disappear because you attended a service. It dies as you submit to truth, renew the mind, and obey the King.

"And be not conformed to this world: but be ye transformed by the renewing of your mind…" (Romans 12:2, KJV)

So this chapter is not about hype. It is not about self-esteem. It is not about motivational identity language.

It is about government - because identity is rebuilt where government is real.

Government is not church politics. It is not man's hierarchy. It is not "because I'm the pastor." God's government means His voice rules you. His Word defines your boundaries. His correction restores you. His order stabilizes you. And under the New Covenant, that government is personal: Christ is the Mediator, the King is accessible, and every believer is responsible to hear and obey.

"My sheep hear my voice, and I know them, and they follow me." (John 10:27, KJV)

Until you come back under the King's government, you will keep trying to rebuild identity with feelings. But when you come back under His rule, shame loses its throne. Babylon loses its grip. And the new man becomes more than a concept - he becomes your operating system.

The King Sets the Boundaries

Shepherds do not set the boundaries of the sheep.

The King does.

"The LORD is our judge, the LORD is our lawgiver, the LORD is our king; he will save us." (Isaiah 33:22, KJV)

That is government stated plainly. God is not one voice among many. He is not a consultant. He is Judge, Lawgiver, and King. That means boundaries are not negotiated by personalities, committees, traditions, or church culture. Boundaries are established by the King through His Word.

"There is one lawgiver, who is able to save and to destroy…" (James 4:12, KJV)

So when a leader tries to build a private fence around the flock - rules God never commanded, restrictions Scripture never required, control disguised as "wisdom" - that is not government. That is man.

Man-made boundaries always produce one of two results: bondage or rebellion. Bondage makes people fear men more than God. Rebellion rises when people have been fed counterfeit authority for so long that they eventually reject authority altogether.

God's boundaries were never designed to suffocate you. They were designed to keep you alive.

"All scripture is given by inspiration of God, and is profitable for doctrine, for reproof, for correction, for instruction in righteousness: That the man of God may be perfect, throughly furnished unto all good works." (2 Timothy 3:16–17, KJV)

That is the boundary system of the Kingdom: doctrine, reproof, correction, instruction. Scripture trains identity by defining what is true, exposing what is false, correcting what is crooked, and instructing what is righteous. And when identity is rebuilt, it is rebuilt inside that boundary - not outside of it.

So hear this clearly:

If a shepherd leads you inside Scripture, he is serving the King. If a shepherd leads you outside Scripture, he is building a private kingdom.

That is why identity restoration requires a final authority. Not your emotions. Not your trauma. Not your preferences. Not a man's title.

The King sets the boundaries. And the sheep become safe when they stay inside the King's fence.

My Sheep Hear My Voice

God's government is not sustained by slogans. It is sustained by hearing.

"My sheep hear my voice, and I know them, and they follow me." (John 10:27, KJV)

That is not poetic language. That is identity definition. Sheep are marked by one thing: they recognize the voice of the Shepherd and respond with obedience.

This is why Babylon thrives where discernment is weak. Babylon does not need to defeat the Church with persecution. It only needs to replace hearing with dependence - dependence on personalities, dependence on platforms, dependence on the mood of a room.

But the Kingdom is built differently.

The King governs His people by His Word and His Spirit. Under the New Covenant, God does not merely command from a distance - He writes His law within.

"I will put my laws into their mind, and write them in their hearts…" (Hebrews 8:10, KJV)

So identity is rebuilt when you stop living by external pressure and start living by internal government - where the Spirit and the Word rule your choices, your reactions, your relationships, and your obedience.

And here is the boundary that must be said plainly: listening to God's voice is not the same as surrendering your conscience to men.

Human hierarchy is still made of men who can sin. Leaders can be right, and leaders can be wrong. Leaders can shepherd, and leaders can manipulate. Leaders can be servants, and leaders can drift into control. That is why God never designed His people to be spiritually deaf - waiting for a human intermediary to tell them what God thinks.

Christ is the Mediator.

"For there is one God, and one mediator between God and men, the man Christ Jesus." (1 Timothy 2:5, KJV)

Access is open.

"Having therefore, brethren, boldness to enter into the holiest by the blood of Jesus…" (Hebrews 10:19, KJV)

That means your identity cannot be built on a man's stability. It must be built on the King's voice.

So when someone tries to rule you with: "Because I said so," while refusing Scripture, refusing accountability, and refusing correction - that is not Kingdom government. That is a counterfeit throne.

Any leader who must keep announcing, "I'm in charge," sounds like the bad boss who must keep saying, "I'm the boss." The words become proof of insecurity. Real authority is not maintained by declaration. It is maintained by alignment.

In the Kingdom, authority is carried by servants who are submitted first - submitted to God, submitted to Scripture, submitted to correction, submitted to accountability.

And the sheep must be trained to hear the King so they are not trapped under the wrong voice.

Shepherds Steward Boundaries

The King sets the boundaries.

Shepherds steward them.

A shepherd is not a king. A shepherd does not own the flock. A shepherd does not invent the standard. A shepherd serves the King by feeding, guarding, and guiding the sheep within the King's fence.

"Feed the flock of God which is among you, taking the oversight thereof… not as being lords over God's heritage, but being ensamples to the flock." (1 Peter 5:2–3, KJV)

That is the job: feed, oversee, and exemplify - without domination.

True shepherding is practical and protective. Shepherds move sheep field to field for a reason: sheep can get sick if they remain too long in one place. Pasture can be destroyed if the flock stays until everything is stripped. And sheep can be harmed if they drink unsafe water.

So the shepherd leads the flock to fresh pasture and safe water - not because the shepherd is controlling, but because the shepherd is responsible.

He guides so they do not destroy what feeds them. He moves them so they do not get sick. He protects them so they do not get devoured.

This is what oversight is supposed to look like. Not religious control. Not personality domination. Stewardship.

And part of stewardship is confronting what poisons the flock: sin.

Hebrews 13:17 defines oversight with accountability:

"…for they watch for your souls, as they that must give account…" (Hebrews 13:17, KJV)

That means shepherds are watchers, not mediators. Servants, not gatekeepers. Stewards, not owners. They watch because sin spreads, deception spreads, bitterness spreads, offense spreads - and the flock must be protected.

But watch what real shepherds do not do:

They do not protect sin because someone is gifted. They do not platform known sin because the person is useful. They do not allow influence to multiply corruption.

Because that is not feeding the flock. That is poisoning it.

And this is where identity rebuilding becomes tangible: your identity is not rebuilt by being "used." It is rebuilt by being made clean, restored, and trained under truth. A shepherd who loves the sheep will confront what is killing them, not showcase what is destroying them.

So yes - shepherds lead field to field and water to water. But they also confront sin that is plaguing the flock, because government is not only comfort. Government is correction.

Sheep Have Teeth

God did not design His people to be helpless.

Sheep are not predators, but they are not powerless. God built defense into the flock - teeth and horns - because the body is supposed to protect the body. Saints are not called to be passive consumers. They are called to be discerning, sober, and resistant to wolves.

That is why God equips the saints. (Ephesians 4:12)

Because an unequipped church becomes dependent. And a dependent church becomes easy to control.

But an equipped church can discern.

"Beloved, believe not every spirit, but try the spirits whether they are of God..." (1 John 4:1, KJV)

So when leadership refuses submission to God - when it refuses Scripture, refuses correction, refuses accountability - the sheep are not commanded to participate in that rebellion. Loyalty to a title is not loyalty to Christ.

Jesus warned what happens when the wrong voice leads.

"Let them alone: they be blind leaders of the blind. And if the blind lead the blind, both shall fall into the ditch." (Matthew 15:14, KJV)

That verse is not permission to become lawless. It is permission to stop following blindness.

Because God's government is still government. Christ is still King. The Word is still the boundary. If a leader will not submit to God, the flock is not obligated to pretend that rebellion is "covering."

And here is the hard truth: some leaders use authority language to mask insecurity.

Anytime a man has to keep saying, "I'm the pastor, I'm in charge," he is functioning like the bad boss who keeps saying, "I'm the boss." The announcement becomes proof of the problem. If authority must be demanded, it is already compromised.

In the Kingdom, leaders lead by alignment. They lead by example. They lead by accountability. They lead by service.

Sheep do not exist to protect leaders from accountability. Leaders exist to protect sheep from deception and sin.

So sheep having teeth means this: the body must be trained to resist wolves, refuse manipulation, and protect the flock - especially the weak - by staying inside Scripture and under Christ's government. Full-grown sheep, ewes, and rams will use their horns, hooves, and teeth to protect the flock from harmful or abusive leaders and predators. They are supposed to do that. It is part of their God-designed nature. They will strike, resist, and, if necessary, kill a bad shepherd.

Do Not Platform Sin

Gifting does not outrank holiness.

A person can be talented and still be toxic. A person can be anointed and still be ungoverned. A person can carry a gift and still carry sin that is plaguing the flock. And when a house ignores sin because a gift is useful, the house trains people to honor performance over purity.

That is not mercy.

That is reinforcement.

"Know ye not that a little leaven leaveneth the whole lump?" (1 Corinthians 5:6, KJV)

Leaven spreads. It does not stay private. It multiplies through contact. Influence is contact at scale. So when you put a person in front of people while known sin is active, you are not "using the gift" - you are multiplying the leaven.

This is why Scripture commands restraint in recognition and elevation.

"Lay hands suddenly on no man…" (1 Timothy 5:22, KJV)

Sudden platforming is reckless. It creates spiritual authority where character has not been proven. It rewards what should be corrected. It pressures the flock to celebrate someone the shepherd should be restoring.

A shepherd does not display what is diseased. A shepherd heals what is diseased.

That does not mean a person is forever disqualified. It means government must be honored: sin confronted, repentance verified, fruit observed, and then function restored in order.

Because if you put someone with active private sin into public display, it will become public. Influence has a way of exposing what was hidden. And when it becomes public, the damage is wider because the stage multiplied the impact.

So the order is simple and non-negotiable:

Confront sin first. Verify repentance. Confirm fruit.

Restore function in order.

Anything else is not restoration. It is compromise.

Public Sin vs Private Sin

God's government does not operate on chaos. It operates on order - even in correction.

Confrontation must be righteous, measured, and obedient to Scripture, or it becomes accusation and carnality.

Jesus gave the pattern:

"Moreover if thy brother shall trespass against thee, go and tell him his fault between thee and him alone..." (Matthew 18:15, KJV)

That is private confrontation first. Not because sin is small, but because God values restoration and does not use unnecessary shame as a tool. If a matter can be resolved privately, it should be.

But Jesus also makes clear that escalation exists when repentance is refused:

"But if he will not hear thee, then take with thee one or two more..." (Matthew 18:16, KJV) *"And if he shall neglect to hear them, tell it unto the church..."* (Matthew 18:17, KJV)

So Scripture recognizes levels of exposure based on levels of refusal.

That brings us to the other side: some sin cannot stay private because it is already damaging the body.

"Them that sin rebuke before all, that others also may fear." (1 Timothy 5:20, KJV)

That is not cruelty. That is protection. Public rebuke is not for private pride - it is for public safety. It establishes fear of God in the house and stops leaven from spreading.

Here is the principle that holds both passages together:

- **Private sin is confronted privately** when it is truly contained and repentance is possible without broader harm.

- **Public sin is addressed publicly** when it has become visible, influential, or destructive to the body - or when refusal to repent forces escalation.

But there is a warning that must be stated plainly: private sin is never safe to platform.

If a person is living in private sin and you put them in front of people, you are not hiding corruption. You are multiplying it. The stage does not cover sin. It spreads its reach. And when exposure comes, the damage is wider because influence widened the blast radius.

That is why God's government insists on order:

- restore the person before showcasing the person,

- heal the wound before assigning influence,

- confirm fruit before releasing visibility.

Because identity is rebuilt in truth, not in performance. And the Church cannot rebuild identity while rewarding what God is trying to confront.

Conclusion: Identity Is Protected by Government

Identity is not rebuilt by being told you are free.

Identity is rebuilt when you come back under the King's rule.

The King sets the boundaries (Isaiah 33:22). His Word defines what is true, what is clean, and what is righteous (2 Timothy 3:16–17). And under the New Covenant, God's government is not mediated through gatekeepers - Christ is the only mediator (1 Timothy 2:5), and the sheep are called to hear His voice (John 10:27).

That is why identity collapses when people surrender discernment to sinful hierarchies. Leaders can serve the flock, but they cannot replace the King. Shepherds steward the King's boundaries, move the flock to health, and confront what poisons the sheep (1 Peter 5:2–3; Hebrews 13:17). And the flock is not designed to be helpless. Sheep have teeth. The body must discern, resist wolves, and refuse blind leadership (1 John 4:1; Matthew 15:14).

This is also why holiness cannot be negotiated for usefulness. Gifting does not outrank righteousness. Leaven spreads (1 Corinthians 5:6). You do not platform known sin and call it ministry. You confront sin first, verify repentance, confirm fruit, and then restore function in order (1 Timothy 5:22). Correction follows Scripture's pattern - private where possible, public where necessary for protection (Matthew 18:15–17; 1 Timothy 5:20).

So here is the chapter's final line:

Identity is rebuilt where government is real. And government is real where Christ rules - not men.

256

Scripture Index

- 2 Corinthians 5:17
- Romans 12:2
- Isaiah 33:22
- James 4:12
- 2 Timothy 3:16–17
- John 10:27
- Hebrews 8:10
- 1 Timothy 2:5
- Hebrews 10:19–22
- 1 Peter 5:2–3
- Hebrews 13:17
- Ephesians 4:12
- 1 John 4:1
- Matthew 15:14
- 1 Corinthians 5:6
- 1 Timothy 5:22
- Matthew 18:15–17
- 1 Timothy 5:20

Chapter Fifteen

Why Mixing Kingdoms Always Corrupts the Church

Introduction: Two Kingdoms Cannot Share a Throne

The Kingdom of God was never designed to coexist peacefully with the kingdoms of men. It was designed to rule them.

There are only two kingdoms operating in the earth. Not three. Not a neutral zone in between. Not a "safe middle" where you can blend loyalties without consequence.

There is the Kingdom of God. And there is the kingdom of this world.

Every person, every institution, every government, every system, every ideology exists under the authority of one or the other - whether they admit it or not. The conflict is not primarily political. It is not cultural. It is not philosophical.

It is governmental.

Scripture never presents the Kingdom of God as a parallel option meant to live alongside earthly systems. It presents it as a superior government that confronts, exposes, judges, and ultimately replaces them. The Kingdom of God does not negotiate its authority. It does not seek permission. It does not adapt to survive. It arrives, confronts, and rules.

Jesus did not come to reform Rome. He came to overthrow its spiritual authority.

"Jesus answered, My kingdom is not of this world: if my kingdom were of this world, then would my servants fight… but now is my kingdom not from hence." (John 18:36, KJV)

That statement was not weakness. It was jurisdiction.

Jesus was not saying His Kingdom had no authority on earth. He was saying it did not originate from earthly systems, and therefore could not be governed by them. Earthly kingdoms rule by force, fear, and coercion. The Kingdom of God rules by truth, authority, obedience, and alignment.

And because of that, the two kingdoms are always in conflict.

The Lie of Coexistence

The Church has been seduced by a lie: that the Kingdom of God can be blended with the kingdom of this world without consequence.

That lie sounds wise. It sounds strategic. It sounds like "balance." But it is rebellion dressed as prudence.

Because two kingdoms cannot share a throne.

"No man can serve two masters…" (Matthew 6:24, KJV)

Jesus did not say it would be difficult. He said it would be impossible. Serving two masters always produces divided loyalty, compromised obedience, and a conscience trained to negotiate truth.

This is why every attempt to mix Kingdom government with worldly systems produces the same result: corruption without repentance.

Daniel was shown this in prophetic form:

"And whereas thou sawest the feet and toes, part of potters' clay, and part of iron, the kingdom shall be divided… but they shall not cleave one to another, even as iron is not mixed with clay." (Daniel 2:41–43, KJV)

Iron represents strength and authority. Clay represents man - weakness, instability, and self-rule.

When divine authority is mixed with human ambition, the structure may look strong, but it is unstable. It cannot stand. It will always fracture under weight because the materials cannot bond. They do not cleave.

That is the modern church crisis in one image: iron mixed with clay.

The Kingdom of God does not need endorsement from the kingdoms of men. It does not need cultural permission to preach truth. It does not need political power to accomplish spiritual mandate.

The moment the Church borrows power from the world, it forfeits spiritual authority. Because the world never funds righteousness without demanding compromise as the price.

"Know ye not that the friendship of the world is enmity with God?" (James 4:4, KJV)

That is not emotional language. It is governmental language.

Friendship means alignment. Partnership. Agreement. Shared direction.

And Scripture calls that enmity - hostility - against God.

So the lie of coexistence always ends the same way: the Church becomes divided, diluted, and domesticated. It keeps its vocabulary but loses its authority. It keeps its activity but loses its fear of God. It keeps its platforms but loses its power to produce repentance.

Because you cannot mix kingdoms without losing one.

Why Mixing Kingdoms Always Corrupts the Church

Mixing kingdoms is not "wisdom." It is corruption.

Because every system carries a spirit. And when the Church tries to borrow the world's methods, the Church also inherits the world's motives: image, influence, control, money, and survival.

The Kingdom of God is built on obedience. The kingdom of this world is built on self-preservation.

So when you mix them, obedience becomes negotiable.

That is why the Church can keep Christian language while losing Kingdom authority. It can keep worship while losing holiness. It can keep preaching while losing repentance. The outside remains, but the government changes.

And the change shows up in one place first: truth becomes adjustable.

When a Church is aligned with God, truth is a boundary. When a Church is aligned with the world, truth becomes a strategy.

That is how Babylon works. Babylon doesn't need you to deny God. It only needs you to edit God.

"To whom ye yield yourselves servants to obey, his servants ye are to whom ye obey..." (Romans 6:16, KJV)

That verse exposes the real master. Your master is not what you claim. Your master is what you obey.

So when the Church yields to the world's demands - its approval systems, its fear of backlash, its obsession with reputation - it has already chosen a master. And once that master is chosen, the Church begins to preach a gospel that can survive in that system.

But the Gospel of the Kingdom was never designed to survive in Babylon. It was designed to judge it.

And judgment begins in the house of God - not because God is harsh, but because God is holy.

"For the time is come that judgment must begin at the house of God..." (1 Peter 4:17, KJV)

So when the Church mixes kingdoms, God doesn't applaud the "strategy." He weighs it. He exposes it. He disciplines it - because a mixed house cannot carry Glory. A divided foundation cannot hold weight.

A mixed church never produces clean fruit. It fills rooms without making disciples, creates motion and activity without carrying authority, raises leaders who are never truly weighed, and offers comfort where correction should have come first. That is the evidence of mixture. It may look alive in public, but its fruit exposes the corruption in the root.

And when correction is removed, corruption multiplies - quietly at first, then openly.

Because the Kingdom of God cannot be built with Babylon's bricks.

The Cost of Choosing the Wrong Kingdom

Kingdom choice is not theoretical. It is measurable.

Every time a church or a believer chooses alignment with the world to preserve comfort, influence, or reputation, something is forfeited. The loss may not be immediate, but it is inevitable.

You cannot protect influence and preserve holiness at the same time if the price of influence is compromise.

Jesus did not present the Kingdom as a negotiation. He presented it as a demand.

"Repent: for the kingdom of heaven is at hand." (Matthew 4:17, KJV)

Repentance is not adjustment. It is surrender. It is a complete turn from one government to another. It is renouncing one throne and submitting to another.

That is why Kingdom preaching produces division.

"Think not that I am come to send peace on earth: I came not to send peace, but a sword." (Matthew 10:34, KJV)

The sword is not violence. It is separation. It divides allegiance. It exposes loyalty. It reveals which kingdom a person truly serves.

When the Church refuses that division, it chooses comfort over clarity. It chooses coexistence over confrontation. It chooses survival over obedience.

And the result is predictable: the Church begins to resemble the world it is trying to influence.

Paul warned this clearly:

"And be not conformed to this world..." (Romans 12:2, KJV)

Conformity is subtle. It rarely begins with denial of truth. It begins with softening. With strategic silence. With selective emphasis. With avoiding offense.

But the Kingdom was never designed to be inoffensive to rebellion.

When the Church tries to protect its seat at the table of worldly power, it forgets something essential: the Kingdom does not need a seat at the table. It overturns tables.

"And Jesus went into the temple of God, and cast out all them that sold and bought in the temple…" (Matthew 21:12, KJV)

He did not negotiate corruption in the Temple. He confronted it. Because the house of God cannot host mixture without losing authority.

Choosing the wrong kingdom always costs more than it promises. It promises relevance. It delivers dilution. It promises influence. It delivers impotence.

Because when you choose the world's approval, you lose the fear of God.

The Remnant Cannot Be Mixed

God has always preserved a remnant - not a crowd.

A remnant is not the group that shouts the loudest. It is the group that remains aligned when compromise becomes normal.

In Babylon, mixture is celebrated. In the Kingdom, mixture is judged - because mixture always produces double-mindedness.

"A double minded man is unstable in all his ways." (James 1:8, KJV)

Instability is not just emotional. It is governmental. A double-minded person cannot hold weight because their obedience is negotiable. And when a house becomes double-minded, it may still have activity - but it loses authority.

That is why the remnant must be separated.

"Wherefore come out from among them, and be ye separate, saith the Lord... and touch not the unclean thing..." (2 Corinthians 6:17, KJV)

Separation is not arrogance. It is protection. It is not hatred of people. It is hatred of mixture.

God does not separate you because He wants you isolated. He separates you because He wants you governed.

Because you cannot build a Kingdom house while living under Babylon's operating system.

No one drifts into holiness. No one drifts into maturity. No one drifts into government.

Drifting always moves toward Babylon - because Babylon is the default current of a fallen world.

That is why the remnant must decide:

Who rules my thinking? Who rules my speech? Who rules my priorities? Who rules my obedience?

Because the Kingdom of God is not carried by those who agree with truth. It is carried by those who **obey** it.

"And why call ye me, Lord, Lord, and do not the things which I say?" (Luke 6:46, KJV)

That is the dividing line.

The remnant is not the people who say "Lord." The remnant is the people who live like He is Lord.

Conclusion: One Kingdom Will Remain

History does not end in coexistence.

It ends in replacement.

Daniel did not see a statue slowly improved. He saw a stone cut without hands strike the image and crush it.

"Thou sawest till that a stone was cut out without hands… which smote the image upon his feet… and brake them to pieces." (Daniel 2:34, KJV)

"And the stone that smote the image became a great mountain, and filled the whole earth." (Daniel 2:35, KJV)

That stone is the Kingdom of God.

It does not integrate. It does not merge. It does not negotiate. It replaces.

Every earthly kingdom will fall. Every cultural system will fade. Every mixed structure will fracture. But the Kingdom that is born of heaven will expand until it fills the earth.

"And in the days of these kings shall the God of heaven set up a kingdom, which shall never be destroyed…" (Daniel 2:44, KJV)

So the issue is not whether the Kingdom will win.

The issue is whether you are aligned with it.

Because you cannot live divided forever. You cannot speak Kingdom and live Babylon indefinitely. One will eventually expose the other.

The Church must decide:

- Will we seek relevance in Babylon?
- Or will we remain governed by the King?

Because one Kingdom will remain. And everything mixed will fall.

Scripture Index

- John 18:36
- Matthew 6:24
- Daniel 2:41–44
- James 4:4
- Romans 6:16
- 1 Peter 4:17
- Matthew 4:17
- Matthew 10:34
- Romans 12:2
- Matthew 21:12
- James 1:8
- 2 Corinthians 6:17
- Luke 6:46

Chapter Sixteen

Sin No More

Introduction: Freedom Is Not Declared, It Is Maintained

Freedom in the Kingdom is not a moment you remember and then assume will keep ruling by itself.

It is not a prayer prayed once, a tear shed once, or a day marked in memory and then revisited as proof that everything is still secure. Freedom is not sustained by remembrance.

Freedom is sustained through obedience.

Freedom is sustained by government.

That is where many fail to discern the difference between mercy and liberty. Mercy may interrupt judgment. Mercy may lift shame. Mercy may open the door. But if the government of God is not established where bondage once ruled, the old pattern will come looking for reentry.

Back doors of compromise must be closed.

What was cast out must not be welcomed back in.

The Kingdom does not just cast demons out.

It keeps them out.

That is why Jesus did not speak as though forgiveness finished the matter.

"Neither do I condemn thee: go, and sin no more." (John 8:11 KJV)

First condemnation is removed.

Then government speaks.

Mercy opens the door, but rule determines whether liberty remains.

Mercy does not cover sin so you can keep it.

Mercy exposes sin so you can be freed from it.

Jesus did not come to improve your coping mechanisms.

He came to break the authority behind them.

"For sin shall not have dominion over you: for ye are not under the law, but under grace." (Romans 6:14, KJV)

Grace is not permission to continue.

Grace is power to stop.

Grace is government restored.

Forgiveness is not the same as freedom. Temporary relief is not permanent liberty. Whatever is not kept under the government of God will eventually drift back toward bondage.

Because in the Kingdom, freedom is not merely declared.

It is maintained.

Forgiveness Is Not the Same as Freedom

Forgiveness removes guilt.

Freedom removes rule.

Confuse those two, and people will call mercy liberty while bondage is still breathing underneath.

That confusion has damaged many. A person comes to God, confesses sin, feels the weight lift, and assumes the matter is finished because condemnation has lifted. But lifted condemnation is not the same thing as broken dominion. Mercy may have opened the door, but if the inward man is not brought under the rule of Christ, the old ruler will try to reclaim ground.

That is why Jesus spoke like a King, not a counselor.

"Neither do I condemn thee: go, and sin no more." (John 8:11, KJV)

Notice the order.

First, condemnation is removed.

Then the command comes.

Mercy clears the record, but government establishes the future.

Jesus did not say, "You are forgiven, so nothing else matters."

He said, in effect, "You are released. Now do not return to what was destroying you."

Scripture is plain.

"For sin shall not have dominion over you: for ye are not under the law, but under grace." (Romans 6:14, KJV)

Dominion is a rulership word.

Grace does not excuse that rulership.

Grace breaks it.

Grace is not permission to continue.

Grace is power to stop.

Grace is government restored.

Mercy is not the end of the matter.

Mercy is the opening for government.

Mercy exposes sin so you can be freed from it.

That means a person can be forgiven and still leave doors open.

Forgiven and still protect an appetite.

Forgiven and still remain inwardly undecided.

Mercy can be real while freedom is still unfinished.

The issue is always yielding.

"Know ye not, that to whom ye yield yourselves servants to obey, his servants ye are to whom ye obey..." (Romans 6:16, KJV)

You do not belong to what you claim.

You belong to what you obey.

Forgiveness addresses guilt before God.

Freedom addresses who rules you now.

And freedom remains only where the rule of sin is broken and the rule of Christ stays in place.

Temporary Relief Is Not Permanent Liberty

Temporary relief can feel like freedom if you do not know the difference.

Pain lifts. Pressure eases. The atmosphere changes. Tears stop. The craving backs off for a moment. And people call that freedom because something broke in the moment.

But not everything that breaks in a moment stays broken.

That is the danger.

Relief changes what you feel.

Liberty changes what rules you.

Relief interrupts pressure.

Liberty breaks the throne behind the pressure.

Jesus made that distinction plain.

"Whosoever drinketh of this water shall thirst again: But whosoever drinketh of the water that I shall give him shall never thirst…" (John 4:13–14, KJV)

Natural water could quiet thirst for a moment, but it could not change the ruler behind the thirst.

Only Christ could do that.

Patterns are sustained by thirst.

Bondage is sustained by agreement.

Freedom is sustained by government.

That is why temporary relief is so deceptive. It gives people enough improvement to avoid full surrender. Enough comfort to keep negotiating with darkness. Enough change to think they no longer need governmental change.

But if the thirst returns, the ruler is still speaking.

If the pattern returns, the agreement was never fully broken.

If the door reopens, the house was never fully governed.

Scripture warns against shallow healing.

"They have healed also the hurt of the daughter of my people slightly, saying, Peace, peace; when there is no peace." (Jeremiah 6:14, KJV)

Something may shift without the root being judged.

Something may calm down while the throne behind it still stands.

Deliverance is not just what happens at the altar.

It is how you live after the altar.

Deliverance is a doorway, but discipleship is the path.

Some want the demon gone but not the discipline.

Freedom without formation becomes a revolving door.

That is why Christ did not come merely to provide relief.

He came to establish liberty under His rule.

The Kingdom Pattern: Government Maintains Freedom

The Kingdom does not maintain freedom through emotion.

It maintains freedom through obedience.

It maintains freedom through government.

That is the pattern many resist. People want freedom without structure, deliverance without discipleship, and Christ as Rescuer without Christ as Ruler. That is why many lose what they once celebrated. They had a moment of breakthrough, but they did not submit to the government that preserves breakthrough.

Scripture is plain.

"If ye continue in my word, then are ye my disciples indeed; And ye shall know the truth, and the truth shall make you free." (John 8:31–32, KVJ)

Notice the order.

Continue.

Then know.

Then be made free.

Freedom is tied to continuation.

Truth does not merely inspire.

Truth rules.

And where truth rules, lies lose power.

That is why freedom cannot be maintained by occasional agreement with God. It must be maintained by ongoing submission. A person who visits truth in crisis but returns to self-rule afterward should not be surprised when bondage returns.

The pattern has always been this plain: what God frees, God also orders.

When Israel came out of Egypt, deliverance was not the finish line.

It was the beginning of government.

God led them to expose what still remained in them that agreed with bondage.

"And thou shalt remember all the way which the Lord thy God led thee these forty years in the wilderness, to humble thee, and to prove thee, to know what was in thine heart..." (Deuteronomy 8:2, KJV)

People can leave Egypt physically and still carry Egypt inwardly.

And inward Egypt will sabotage outward deliverance.

That is why the government is not punishment.

Government is preservation.

Freedom that is not governed will not remain free.

Some want the demon gone but not the discipline.

If the house is not filled with truth, the old spirits return with reinforcements.

The Kingdom does more than expel what is unclean; it establishes what is holy.

It keeps them out.

Government shuts the door.

Freedom is maintained by remaining under what God says now.

Where government remains, freedom remains.

Hidden Agreements Reopen Bondage

Bondage does not always return through open rebellion.

Many times it returns through hidden agreement.

A hidden agreement is any place where your mouth says one thing, but your inner permission says another. You say you want freedom, but you still protect the appetite that enslaved you. You say you belong to God, but you still keep room for the fantasy, the offense, the compromise, or the idol.

That is why Scripture is sharp about the inner life.

"Keep thy heart with all diligence; for out of it are the issues of life." (Proverbs 4:23, KJV)

The heart is not neutral ground.

It is a government center.

What you protect there will eventually speak through your life.

This is where many lose freedom. They stop the behavior for a season, but never judge the agreement beneath it. They cut off the fruit, but keep watering the root. They remove the visible pattern, but leave the inner permission alive.

And hidden permission always reopens visible bondage.

That is why Paul said:

"Neither give place to the devil." (Ephesians 4:27, KJV)

Place means room.

Ground.

Opportunity.

The enemy does not need your public announcement.

He needs your private opening.

The offense you keep nursing.

The compromise you keep excusing.

The lie you keep tolerating.

The wound you keep enthroning above truth.

Provision is agreement made practical.

What you keep feeding, you keep strengthening.

What you keep strengthening will eventually demand rule.

Hidden agreements are doors.

And doors do not stay harmless because they are private.

"Casting down imaginations, and every high thing that exalteth itself against the knowledge of God, and bringing into captivity every thought to the obedience of Christ." (2 Corinthians 10:5, KJV)

That is war language.

Whatever is left unjudged inwardly will eventually resist God outwardly.

You cannot stay free while secretly admiring what God calls unclean.

You cannot stay free while privately defending what truth has already judged.

You cannot stay free while inwardly keeping a treaty with the thing Christ came to destroy.

Because what you hide, you protect.

And what you protect, you empower.

And what you empower will eventually try to rule you again.

Hardcore Example: When Hidden Sin Becomes Public

This is how it happens.

A man builds a public ministry, a public image, a public voice. People call it anointing because something moves in the room. Something seems alive. But behind the curtain, the private life is being governed by something else. Small compromise is protected by secrecy, justified by pressure, excused by stress, and defended by spiritual language.

And the house keeps moving.

The platform keeps functioning.

The crowd keeps clapping.

But the government is already leaking.

That is the danger of hidden agreement. It does not have to announce itself publicly to be deadly. It only has to remain protected privately. Once a leader keeps secret permission alive with what God has judged, the breach has already begun. The room may still be full. The gift may still appear effective. The system may still look successful. But the inner structure is already weakening.

Then pressure increases.

And pressure always finds the crack.

A private pattern becomes a public exposure.

A private indulgence becomes a public scandal.

And what shocks people is not only what happened.

It is how long it was happening while everything still looked alive.

Scripture warned about this plainly.

"For there is nothing covered, that shall not be revealed; neither hid, that shall not be known." (Luke 12:2, KJV)

Hidden sin is never private.

It is private rebellion with public consequences.

Families are hit.

Trust collapses.

Sheep become suspicious of authority itself because counterfeit authority always poisons the category it imitates.

"Be sure your sin will find you out." (Numbers 32:23, KJV)

That is not poetry.

That is law.

Law does not bend for gifting, titles, crowds, or image. If sin is protected, it will eventually speak.

What was hidden in private will eventually bill the house in public.

But the Kingdom does not preserve image.

The Kingdom preserves holiness.

"He that covereth his sins shall not prosper: but whoso confesseth and forsaketh them shall have mercy." (Proverbs 28:13, KJV)

Mercy is promised to confession and forsaking, not to concealment and management.

The only safe way is light.

Light Is the Only Safe Way to Stay Free

Freedom cannot be maintained in darkness.

Not because God is cruel.

Because darkness protects what God is trying to kill.

That is why light is not optional in the Kingdom. Light is not a personality trait for unusually transparent people. Light is the only safe environment for freedom because only light keeps lies from rebuilding their throne.

Scripture is plain.

"But if we walk in the light, as he is in the light, we have fellowship one with another, and the blood of Jesus Christ his Son cleanseth us from all sin." (1 John 1:7, KJV)

Notice the language.

Walk in the light.

Not visit the light.

Not run to the light only after collapse.

Walk in the light.

Light is meant to be the climate you live in so bondage does not keep rebuilding.

This is where many sabotage their own freedom. They want cleansing without exposure, help without honesty, prayer without truth. But the blood of Jesus is not joined to darkness. Cleansing works where truth is welcomed, lies are broken, and the soul comes out of hiding.

"If we say that we have no sin, we deceive ourselves, and the truth is not in us." (1 John 1:8, KJV)

Deception grows where honesty dies.

That is why confession is not weakness.

It is warfare.

"Confess your faults one to another, and pray one for another, that ye may be healed." (James 5:16, KJV)

Healing is joined to truthfulness.

Secrecy is the incubator of bondage.

Light is the atmosphere where bondage begins to suffocate.

That old thought pattern?

Crucify it.

That toxic relationship?

Sever it.

That secret sin?

Drag it into the light.

And hear this clearly.

The goal of light is not humiliation.

The goal of light is liberty.

God does not expose to destroy the repentant.

He exposes to destroy what has been destroying them.

He exposes because He loves truth in the inward parts.

"Behold, thou desirest truth in the inward parts..." (Psalm 51:6, KJV)

Stay in the light.

Stay honest.

Stay searchable.

Stay open to correction before correction has to become exposure.

Because light is not merely how freedom begins.

Light is how freedom stays free.

Conclusion - Freedom Remains Where Government Remains

Freedom does not remain because a person once had an experience.

Freedom remains because the government of God is still ruling what was once in bondage.

That is the line of this chapter. Forgiveness is not the same as freedom. Temporary relief is not permanent liberty. Hidden agreements reopen bondage. Secrecy protects what truth is trying to kill. Light is the only safe way to stay free.

All of it leads to one conclusion:

Freedom remains where government remains.

That is why shallow religion cannot preserve liberty. Religion can manage appearances while the inner man stays compromised. It can celebrate moments while ignoring the structures that keep a soul aligned. But the Kingdom is not built on emotional memory.

It is built on present rule.

What Christ frees, Christ intends to govern.

"Stand fast therefore in the liberty wherewith Christ hath made us free..." (Galatians 5:1. KJV)

That command exists because liberty does not maintain itself automatically. Bondage keeps looking for reentry where government weakens. Liberty must be held under the rule of truth.

That is the safe place.

Not gift without order.

Not mercy without repentance.

Not relief without structure.

Not language without obedience.

The safe place is government.

The safe place is where truth rules quickly.

Where hidden agreements are judged early.

Where the inward man stays open to the light of God.

Because freedom is never safest where people feel strongest.

Freedom is safest where God is allowed to govern deepest.

So let this be settled.

Do not merely seek moments.

Seek rule.

Do not merely seek relief.

Do not seek freedom alone; seek the rule that keeps freedom clean.

Seek government.

The Kingdom does not just cast demons out.

It keeps them out.

Government shuts the door.

Because Christ did not come merely to interrupt bondage.

He came to establish dominion over everything bondage once ruled.

And where His government remains, freedom remains.

Scripture Index

- John 4:13–14
- John 8:11
- John 8:31–32
- Luke 12:2
- Romans 6:14
- Romans 6:16
- 2 Corinthians 10:5
- Galatians 5:1
- Ephesians 4:27
- James 5:16
- 1 John 1:7
- 1 John 1:8
- Psalm 51:6
- Proverbs 4:23
- Proverbs 28:13
- Jeremiah 6:14
- Deuteronomy 8:2
- Numbers 32:23

Chapter Seventeen

Walking in Kingdom Authority

Introduction: Authority Is Not Volume, It Is Weight

Kingdom authority is not attitude. It is not volume. It is not the ability to intimidate a room.

Authority is weight - and weight only rests where government is real.

In the Kingdom, authority is never self-generated. You do not "take" it by confidence. You receive it by alignment. You carry it by obedience. You increase in it by faithfulness.

"And Jesus came and spake unto them, saying, All power is given unto me in heaven and in earth." (Matthew 28:18, KJV)

Jesus did not claim authority as a man trying to become something. He carried authority as the Son submitted to the Father's will.

"For I came down from heaven, not to do mine own will, but the will of him that sent me." (John 6:38, KJV)

That is the Kingdom pattern: authority flows through submission, not self-promotion.

This is why many people try to operate in authority and nothing moves - because they are trying to use a Kingdom weapon while living under a different government. They want authority without obedience. They want weight without alignment. They want results while resisting correction.

But authority is measured by fruit, not claims.

"And in thy majesty ride prosperously because of truth and meekness and righteousness…" (Psalm 45:4, KJV)

Truth. Meekness. Righteousness. Not ego. Not control. Not image.

And the boundary is unavoidable: you cannot carry Kingdom authority while protecting sin. The moment sin is tolerated, authority leaks. The moment obedience becomes negotiable, weight reduces. The moment the throne is shared, government is compromised.

This chapter is about walking in Kingdom authority the way Scripture defines it - authority that remains, authority that protects, authority that confronts darkness without becoming darkness, and authority that builds the house instead of building a platform.

Authority Comes From Submission, Not Title

Titles do not create authority. Submission does.

Authority in the Kingdom is not self-appointed. You do not become authoritative because you were handed a microphone, elected to a role, or placed into a position. Authority is the delegated weight of heaven resting on a life that is aligned.

Even Jesus operated this way. He did not function from independence. He functioned from submission.

"For I came down from heaven, not to do mine own will, but the will of him that sent me." (John 6:38, KJV)

That is the pattern. Authority flows through a submitted will.

So when someone tries to speak with authority while living in private rebellion, what comes out may be loud, but it will not be weighty. Volume can be faked. Weight cannot.

The centurion understood this better than most believers do. He recognized that authority is not personality - it is jurisdiction.

"For I am a man under authority… and I say to this man, Go, and he goeth…" (Matthew 8:9, KJV)

Notice what he said first: "under authority." His authority worked because he was submitted to a higher government.

That is why Kingdom authority is impossible to carry while refusing correction. If you cannot be ruled, you cannot rule. If you cannot submit, you cannot be entrusted. If you refuse government, you forfeit weight.

"And why call ye me, Lord, Lord, and do not the things which I say?" (Luke 6:46, KJV)

Calling Him Lord while ignoring His commands is contradiction. It is a claim without alignment. And claims do not move heaven.

Authority is proven by obedience and fruit, not by declaration.

"Ye shall know them by their fruits." (Matthew 7:16, KJV)

Fruit is evidence of government. It reveals who is ruling the life.

Here is the dividing line: a title can put you in front of people, but only submission puts weight behind your words.

And if you want authority to increase, the pathway is not promotion - it is faithfulness.

"He that is faithful in that which is least is faithful also in much…" (Luke 16:10, KJV)

Authority grows where obedience remains.

Hardcore Example - Sons of Sceva: Using Authority Without Government

Some men tried to use the *language* of authority without living under the *government* of authority. They treated Jesus' name like a formula - like a tool they could borrow for results.

"And the evil spirit answered and said, Jesus I know, and Paul I know; but who are ye?" (Acts 19:15, KJV)

"And the man in whom the evil spirit was leaped on them, and overcame them, and prevailed against them, so that they fled out of that house naked and wounded." (Acts 19:16, KJV)

That is what happens when you try to wield Kingdom authority while refusing Kingdom alignment. You can quote the right Name and still lack jurisdiction. Authority is not volume. It is weight. And weight only rests where government remains.

Authority Is Stewardship, Not Ownership

Kingdom authority is never ownership. It is stewardship.

The moment a person treats authority like possession - *my people, my church, my platform, my ministry* - they have already shifted into Babylon logic. In the Kingdom, nothing belongs to the servant. Everything belongs to the King.

"The earth is the LORD's, and the fulness thereof; the world, and they that dwell therein." (Psalm 24:1, KJV)

That includes the sheep.

So spiritual authority is not the right to control people. It is the responsibility to protect people. It is the weight of stewardship - answering to God for how you handled what was entrusted.

"And he said unto him, Well done, thou good servant… thou hast been faithful in a very little, have thou authority…" (Luke 19:17, KJV)

Authority is given as a reward for faithful stewardship, not demanded as a right.

This is why true authority always carries humility. Because the one carrying it knows he is accountable. He knows he will give account. He knows the sheep were never his property.

"Obey them that have the rule over you… for they watch for your souls, as they that must give account…" (Hebrews 13:17, KJV)

Watchers give account. Owners do not. Stewards do.

So when leadership becomes possessive, it becomes abusive. When leadership becomes protective of its image instead of protective of the flock, it becomes dangerous. When leadership starts demanding loyalty to itself instead of loyalty to truth, it has crossed the line from stewardship into domination.

This is why Scripture forbids lordship.

"Neither as being lords over God's heritage, but being ensamples to the flock." (1 Peter 5:3, KJV)

The flock is God's heritage, not yours. You are an example, not a monarch.

So Kingdom authority is stewardship: serving the King by guarding His people, feeding His people, confronting sin that harms His people, and keeping the house aligned with His Word.

And if you forget that, authority leaks. Because God will not empower ownership. He empowers stewardship.

Authority Confronts Darkness Without Becoming It

Kingdom authority confronts darkness, but it does not imitate darkness.

It does not use manipulation to fight manipulation. It does not use intimidation to fight intimidation. It does not use domination to fight domination.

Because the moment you adopt the enemy's methods, you have already compromised the government you claim to represent.

The Kingdom advances by truth.

"And in thy majesty ride prosperously because of truth and meekness and righteousness..." (Psalm 45:4, KJV)

Truth. Meekness. Righteousness.

Jesus had authority because He had alignment. He did not need theatrics. He did not need fear tactics. Demons recognized jurisdiction.

"And he... taught them as one having authority, and not as the scribes." (Matthew 7:29, KJV)

The scribes had information. Jesus had government.

And when He confronted darkness, it moved.

"And he rebuked him, saying, Hold thy peace, and come out of him. And when the devil had thrown him in the midst, he came out of him..." (Luke 4:35, KJV)

But here is the warning: authority leaks when sin is tolerated. You cannot confront darkness publicly while agreeing with darkness privately. Private compromise drains public authority.

"Be ye clean, that bear the vessels of the LORD." (Isaiah 52:11, KJV)

That command is not legalism. It is government. If you carry holy things, you must not protect unholy agreements.

So Kingdom authority confronts darkness, but it does it without becoming harsh, carnal, or controlling. It stays inside truth, meekness, and righteousness - because that is how the King rules.

Authority Is Tested Under Pressure

Authority is not proven in comfort. It is proven under pressure.

Pressure is the proving ground of government.

Because under pressure, your true ruler shows up. Your real master becomes visible. Your actual allegiance is revealed.

No one proves submission when everything is easy. Submission is revealed when obedience costs you something.

"And why call ye me, Lord, Lord, and do not the things which I say?" (Luke 6:46, KJV)

Many people claim authority but collapse when confrontation comes. They want authority to confront demons, but they won't confront sin. They want authority to command atmospheres, but they won't govern appetites. They want authority to speak to mountains, but they won't obey in small things.

"He that is faithful in that which is least is faithful also in much…" (Luke 16:10, KJV)

Authority is built in the "least." In private obedience. In small corrections. In quiet alignment. In resisting compromise when no one is watching.

Pressure does not create compromise. It reveals it.

If a person is already mixed, pressure will expose it. If a person is already aligned, pressure will prove it.

That is why the Kingdom is not moved by claims. It is moved by faithfulness.

And this is also why many houses lose authority: they protect peace instead of protecting truth. They avoid conflict instead of confronting sin. They retreat from correction because it risks attendance.

But authority does not grow where truth is negotiable. Authority grows where obedience remains.

When pressure comes, the question is not, "How do I keep my position?" The question is, "How do I remain aligned with the King?"

Because pressure is the test.

And whatever fails under pressure was never government. It was performance.

Conclusion: Weight Rests Where Government Remains

Kingdom authority is not volume. It is weight.

And weight only rests where government is real - where a life is submitted, aligned, and obedient under the King.

Authority comes from submission, not title (John 6:38). It is stewardship, not ownership (Psalm 24:1). It confronts darkness without becoming darkness - because it advances by truth, meekness, and righteousness (Psalm 45:4). And it is proven under pressure, where faithfulness in the least reveals true government (Luke 16:10).

If you cannot be ruled, you cannot rule. If you refuse correction, you forfeit weight. If you protect sin, authority leaks.

So the path is simple, but it is not soft:

Submit to the King. Stay inside Scripture. Remain clean. Be faithful in the least. Carry stewardship with fear of God.

Then authority will not be a concept you talk about. It will be a weight your life carries.

Scripture Index

- John 6:38
- Matthew 28:18
- Psalm 45:4
- Matthew 8:9
- Luke 6:46
- Matthew 7:16
- Luke 16:10
- Acts 19:15–16
- Psalm 24:1
- Luke 19:17
- Hebrews 13:17
- 1 Peter 5:3

Chapter Eighteen

The House Must Be Clean

Introduction: God Will Not Build on What He Will Judge

God does not pour Glory into what He plans to purge.

He does not strengthen what He must dismantle. He does not endorse what He must expose.

Judgment begins at the house of God (1 Peter 4:17). That is not a threat - it is a mercy. Because if God does not cleanse the house, the house cannot carry weight. And if the house cannot carry weight, it cannot hold what heaven releases.

Many people want authority but refuse cleansing. Many want the River but avoid correction. Many want Kingdom results while protecting private agreements.

But the Kingdom is not built on enthusiasm. It is built on holiness.

"Be ye holy; for I am holy." (1 Peter 1:16, KJV)

Holiness is not religious image. Holiness is separation from what defiles. It is alignment with what God calls clean. And it is not optional - because unclean vessels leak authority.

This chapter is about the cleansing God requires in His people and in His house. Not as performance. Not as shame. As government.

Because God will not build on what He will judge.

Cleansing Is Not Condemnation

Cleansing is not God rejecting you.

Cleansing is God preparing you.

The enemy uses shame to drive you away from God. God uses conviction to bring you back under truth. Shame says, "You are filthy, so hide." Conviction says, "You are defiled, so come into the light."

"If we confess our sins, he is faithful and just to forgive us our sins, and to cleanse us from all unrighteousness." (1 John 1:9, KJV)

Notice the order: forgiveness and cleansing. God does not only pardon. He purifies. He does not only remove guilt. He removes defilement - because defilement cannot carry weight.

This is why the blood of Jesus is not only a legal transaction. It is a cleansing power.

"How much more shall the blood of Christ... purge your conscience from dead works to serve the living God?" (Hebrews 9:14, KJV)

A purged conscience produces service. That is government. When the conscience is cleansed, the will becomes governable. When the will becomes governable, the house becomes stable.

So cleansing is not condemnation. It is preparation.

And this is why judgment begins at the house of God (1 Peter 4:17). God starts with His own house because He intends to dwell there. He intends to build there. He intends to release weight there.

But He will not pour Glory into defilement.

You can have gifting and still be defiled. You can have position and still be defiled. You can have activity and still be defiled.

Defilement is not measured by how loud you worship. It is measured by what you tolerate.

This is why Scripture warns against a form without power.

"Having a form of godliness, but denying the power thereof…" (2 Timothy 3:5, KJV)

The power is not only miracles. The power is cleansing. The power is transformation. The power is holiness. A house that refuses cleansing denies the power that would change it.

So God does not cleanse to humiliate. He cleanses to restore government. He cleanses to protect the flock. He cleanses to keep the house from collapse.

God Judges What He Intends to Inhabit

God does not judge the house because He hates it.

He judges the house because He intends to dwell in it.

Judgment is not always destruction. Often it is purification. The same fire that consumes chaff refines gold. And God is willing to burn what is defiling because He is committed to what He is building.

"For the time is come that judgment must begin at the house of God…" (1 Peter 4:17, KJV)

That verse is not optional. It is a principle of government: God cleanses His dwelling first.

This is why people misunderstand the fear of the Lord. They think fear means terror. But in Scripture, fear means reverence under authority - recognizing that God is not to be handled casually.

"Wherefore we receiving a kingdom which cannot be moved… let us have grace, whereby we may serve God acceptably with reverence and godly fear: For our God is a consuming fire." (Hebrews 12:28–29, KJV)

If God is a consuming fire, then what you tolerate matters. Fire does not negotiate. Fire reveals.

This is also why the veil being torn matters so much. It did not only give access - it removed the ability for men to control access.

"And, behold, the veil of the temple was rent in twain from the top to the bottom…" (Matthew 27:51, KJV)

God tore it from top to bottom. Not man. God removed the priestly barrier so relationship would no longer be filtered through gatekeepers. Access is now in Christ, not in a system.

"Having therefore, brethren, boldness to enter into the holiest by the blood of Jesus…" (Hebrews 10:19, KJV)

So if access is open, defilement becomes the issue. Not distance. Not permission. Not "waiting for a man." The real question is whether the vessel is clean enough to carry what God releases.

And this is where leaders must be honest: church leadership is still made of men who can sin. Some leaders are dealing with sin the same as everyone else. Some hide it. Some manage it. Some are dealing with things worse than the sheep they preach to. That is why God never designed your relationship with Him to be dependent on the stability of a human hierarchy.

Christ is the Head. And the house must be clean.

So God judges what He intends to inhabit. Because He refuses to pour Glory into a house that protects sin. He refuses to strengthen a structure that is already compromised.

Judgment begins here - not to destroy the house, but to make it fit to hold what He is about to release.

The House Leaks Where Sin Is Protected

A house does not collapse only because sin exists.

It collapses because sin is protected.

When sin is confronted, it can be cleansed. When sin is hidden, it multiplies. When sin is excused, it becomes culture.

"Know ye not that a little leaven leaveneth the whole lump?" (1 Corinthians 5:6, KJV)

And Scripture gives a brutal picture of this principle: Achan.

Israel lost a battle they should have won - not because God was weak, but because the camp was defiled. One man hid what God had forbidden, and the whole body paid for one protected secret.

"And the children of Israel committed a trespass in the accursed thing…" (Joshua 7:1, KJV)

"Israel hath sinned… they have even taken of the accursed thing… and have put it even among their own stuff." (Joshua 7:11, KJV)

That is government. Hidden sin is not "personal" when it's inside a covenant people. One protected agreement can shut down public authority. One secret can poison a whole camp. That is why God exposes what is buried - because the house cannot carry weight while it is hiding what heaven already judged.

This is why Scripture commands the Church to deal with sin inside the house with seriousness - not as shame, but as government.

"Do not ye judge them that are within?" (1 Corinthians 5:12, KJV)

Government means there are boundaries. Standards. Consequences. Accountability.

And the most common way a house protects sin is by rewarding gifting over holiness. People are placed in front of the flock while private sin is active because they are "useful." That is not mercy. That is reinforcement. It teaches the sheep that influence outranks purity.

"Lay hands suddenly on no man..." (1 Timothy 5:22, KJV)

That is a boundary. Not suspicion. Not paranoia. Wisdom. Government.

And when sin becomes public - or when a person refuses correction - Scripture is clear:

"Them that sin rebuke before all, that others also may fear." (1 Timothy 5:20, KJV)

Fear of God protects the house.

This is why Jesus confronted religious leaders so harshly. He did not hate them. He hated what they protected. They used religion to hide sin, control people, and protect image. That is why He called them serpents and vipers.

"Ye serpents, ye generation of vipers..." (Matthew 23:33, KJV)

Because a system that protects sin while demanding honor is venomous.

So the house leaks where sin is protected. If you want the house to hold weight, you must remove what creates leaks: secrecy, tolerance, favoritism, and fear of man.

God will not pour glory into a compromised structure. He will cleanse it first.

Hardcore Example: When Government Had to Protect the House From the Priests

Biblical Example: When the Priests Could Not Be Trusted With the House

There are seasons in Scripture when the most frightening corruption in the nation is not found in the palace.

It is found at the altar.

Not because God failed to establish priesthood.

Because men entrusted with holy things learned how to stand near glory while refusing its government.

That is the terror of institutional corruption in the house of God. The leaders charged with guarding the altar, stewarding the money, preserving the order, and maintaining the house become the very men through whom decay is protected. What should have been repaired is neglected. What should have been guarded is exploited. What should have been holy is treated like private property. And the house begins to leak because sin has found sanctuary in the structure itself.

This is exactly what happened in the days of Joash.

The command was clear. The temple needed repair. The priests had responsibility. The resources were there. But the men who should have maintained the house did not do what was required.

"And it came to pass after this, that Joash was minded to repair the house of the Lord. And he gathered together the priests and the Levites, and said to them, Go out unto the cities of Judah, and gather of all Israel money to repair the house of your God from year to year, and see that ye hasten the matter. Howbeit the Levites hastened it not." (2 Chronicles 24:4–5, KJV)

That is not a small failure.

That is leadership rot.

The men closest to the house would not hasten to repair the house.

The men nearest the altar would not move with urgency for the altar.

And the king had to confront them.

"And the king called for Jehoiada the chief, and said unto him, Why hast thou not required of the Levites to bring in out of Judah and out of Jerusalem the collection… for the tabernacle of witness?" (2 Chronicles 24:6, KJV)

Again, Scripture leaves no room for soft language. The issue was not lack of instruction. The issue was failure in those entrusted with the task. So government had to step in. A chest was set outside. A locked collection system was established. The priests were removed from direct handling because trust had already been broken.

"But king Joash called for Jehoiada the priest, and the other priests, and said unto them, Why repair ye not the breaches of the house? now therefore receive no more money of your acquaintance, but deliver it for the breaches of the house. And the priests consented to receive no more money of the people, neither to repair the breaches of the house. But Jehoiada the priest took a chest, and bored a hole in the lid of it, and set it beside the altar…" (2 Kings 12:7–9, KJV)

Do not miss how severe that is.

Government had to protect the house from the priests.

The men claiming spiritual custody could not be trusted with practical stewardship.

The men standing nearest the sacred place had become so unreliable that a control had to be imposed beside the altar itself.

That is not merely an accounting adjustment.

That is judgment on spiritual leadership.

And it happened again in the days of Josiah.

Once more the house needed repair. Once more the order had to be restored. Once more money had to be gathered and work had to be done. But this time the contrast is even sharper. The workmen proved more trustworthy than the priests.

"And they put it in the hand of the workmen that had the oversight of the house of the Lord… Moreover they reckoned not with the men, into whose hand they delivered the money to be bestowed on workmen: for they dealt faithfully." (2 Kings 22:5, 7, KJV)

And again:

"And they delivered the money that was brought into the house of God into the hand of the overseers, and to the hand of the workmen… And the men did the work faithfully." (2 Chronicles 34:10, 12, KJV)

Think about the humiliation of that.

The craftsmen were trusted.

The repairers were trusted.

The workers were trusted.

But the priesthood had already proven so compromised in prior generations that heaven's record highlights the faithfulness of builders rather than the reliability of altar-men.

And after the repairs, there was still money left to make articles for the house, things the priests should have cared for as part of their own calling.

"And when they had finished it, they brought the rest of the money before the king and Jehoiada, whereof were made vessels for the house of the Lord…" (2 Chronicles 24:14, KJV)

That means the issue was never that God failed to provide.

The issue was that spiritual leaders failed to steward.

This is not mainly about private sin.

This is about institutional corruption in the house.

It is about spiritual leaders entrusted with altar, money, maintenance, holiness, and covenant order proving unfaithful physically, morally, and scripturally. It is about men carrying title without carrying weight. Men claiming anointing without submitting to government. Men wanting the people tested while refusing to be tested themselves.

That is the same disease still working now.

Church leaders want to rule like kings while refusing to live like servants.

They want unquestioned access, unquestioned loyalty, unquestioned money, unquestioned authority, and unquestioned motives. They declare themselves anointed and then act insulted when discernment is applied to them. They demand that sheep be examined, corrected, filtered, and broken, but they rage at the thought that their own doctrine, character, use of money, handling of people, and private life should also be weighed.

But Scripture never gave church leaders the right to be self-authenticating.

Civil rulers are openly appointed by God in the order of society.

"Let every soul be subject unto the higher powers. For there is no power but of God: the powers that be are ordained of God." (Romans 13:1, KJV)

That does not make every ruler righteous. But it does mean government exists by divine allowance and carries delegated jurisdiction. And in Scripture there were times when kings trembled more over the house of God than priests who stood beside the altar. Joash and Josiah understood the seriousness of the house while priests treated its maintenance casually. Civil rulers sometimes showed more fear of dishonoring God's house than the men who handled its offerings every day.

That should terrify modern leaders.

Because when priests refuse God's order, heaven will raise other government to expose, restrain, and repair what they have corrupted.

Read that again.

When priests refuse God's order, heaven will raise other government to expose, restrain, and repair what they have corrupted.

That is not rebellion against the house.

That is protection of the house.

Because God judges what He intends to inhabit.

And the house leaks where sin is protected.

So when corrupt spiritual leaders become so compromised that they cannot be trusted with stewardship, heaven does not shrug. Heaven does not call it "just their personality." Heaven does not say, "Leave it alone because they are anointed." Heaven intervenes. Heaven exposes. Heaven restrains. Heaven repairs.

That is what the lockbox by the altar meant.

It meant title was no longer enough.

It meant proximity to sacred things was no longer proof of faithfulness.

It meant the men handling the money could not be trusted merely because they wore priestly garments.

That is the brutal lesson many modern houses still refuse to learn.

Anointing claimed is not anointing proven.

Authority asserted is not authority established.

And leaders who cannot be tested are leaders already drifting toward corruption.

Some church leaders hate that sentence because pride wants priesthood without accountability. Pride wants reverence without examination. Pride wants access without scrutiny. Pride wants kingly treatment from the people while refusing servant-hearted submission to Christ. But New Covenant leadership was not promoted into kingship.

It was demoted into service.

The Lord did not enthrone ministers to be feared.

He made them stewards to be judged by faithfulness.

So let the example stand with full force. There were days in Israel when the priests proved less trustworthy than the craftsmen, less urgent than the king, less faithful than the workers, and less careful with the house than the civil ruler overseeing the repairs.

That is shameful.

That is indictment.

And that is warning.

Because any house that protects corrupt spiritual stewardship is already leaking.

Any altar that cannot examine its own leaders is already compromised.

Any ministry that demands testing for the sheep while refusing testing for the shepherd has already departed from the government of God.

And when that happens, do not be shocked if Heaven raises a rod from outside the structure to restrain what the structure refused to judge from within.

Clean Vessels Carry Weight

God does not entrust weight to leaking vessels.

He entrusts weight to clean vessels - because holiness is not decoration. Holiness is capacity.

If you want to know why many people feel powerless, it is often not because God is distant. It is because the vessel is compromised. The conscience is defiled. The will is divided. The throne is shared.

"How much more shall the blood of Christ… purge your conscience from dead works to serve the living God?" (Hebrews 9:14, KJV)

A purged conscience produces service. A clean conscience produces steadiness. A steady conscience can carry responsibility without collapse.

This is why Scripture connects cleansing with usefulness:

"If a man therefore purge himself from these, he shall be a vessel unto honour, sanctified, and meet for the master's use…" (2 Timothy 2:21, KJV)

Meet for the Master's use means fit - usable - trusted - capable of carrying assignment without corrupting it.

So holiness is not self-righteousness. Holiness is submission to God's standards so your vessel can hold what He releases.

And the cleansing isn't optional because the King is not casual.

"Be ye holy; for I am holy." (1 Peter 1:16, KJV)

When the Lord intends to move, He does not lower His standard to match a weak vessel. He strengthens the vessel by cleansing it.

This is why the fear of the Lord matters. It is not emotional panic. It is reverence under authority.

"Let us have grace, whereby we may serve God acceptably with reverence and godly fear: For our God is a consuming fire." (Hebrews 12:28–29, KJV)

Fire does not negotiate. Fire reveals what is flammable. Fire exposes what is false. Fire proves what is pure.

So if you want to carry Kingdom authority, the pathway is not louder declarations - it is a cleaner life. Not perfectionism. Cleansing. Not image. Government.

Clean vessels carry weight.

Conclusion: God Cleans What He Plans to Fill

God is not reluctant to dwell with His people.

He is unwilling to dwell with what defiles them.

God cleans what He plans to fill.

And He proves it in the New Testament with a fear-of-God moment most people try to skip: Ananias and Sapphira. They wanted the appearance of sacrifice without the reality of truth - hypocrisy protected inside the house.

"But Peter said, Ananias, why hath Satan filled thine heart to lie to the Holy Ghost…?" (Acts 5:3, KJV)

"…Ananias hearing these words fell down, and gave up the ghost…" (Acts 5:5, KJV)

"Then fell she down straightway at his feet, and yielded up the ghost…" (Acts 5:10, KJV)

"And great fear came upon all the church…" (Acts 5:11, KJV)

That is not random tragedy. That is government. God was establishing a clean house, a truthful house, a house that could carry weight. He was showing the early Church: you don't build the Kingdom on protected sin.

Judgment begins at the house of God (1 Peter 4:17) because God intends to inhabit the house. He intends to release weight into it. And weight will not rest on what is leaking.

Cleansing is not condemnation. It is preparation (1 John 1:9). The blood does not only forgive; it purges the conscience so the vessel can serve (Hebrews 9:14). The veil was torn from top to bottom (Matthew 27:51) to remove gatekeeping and restore access - so the issue is no longer distance but defilement (Hebrews 10:19). And because access is open, God's government demands a clean house.

A house leaks where sin is protected. Leaven spreads (1 Corinthians 5:6). Favoritism toward gifting corrupts the flock. Hasty platforming creates spiritual damage (1 Timothy 5:22). And when sin is public or refuses correction, fear of God must protect the body (1 Timothy 5:20). God will not pour Glory into compromise.

But the promise is clear: clean vessels carry weight. When a man purges himself, he becomes fit for the Master's use (2 Timothy 2:21). Holiness becomes capacity, not performance. Cleansing becomes alignment, not shame.

So the conclusion is simple:

God cleans what He plans to fill. And the house that submits to cleansing becomes a house that can hold Glory.

Scripture Index

- 1 Peter 4:17
- 1 Peter 1:16
- 1 John 1:9
- Hebrews 9:14
- 2 Timothy 3:5
- Hebrews 12:28–29
- Matthew 27:51
- Hebrews 10:19
- 1 Corinthians 5:6
- 1 Corinthians 5:12
- 1 Timothy 5:20-22
  Matthew 23:33
- 2 Timothy 2:21
- Joshua 7:1
- Joshua 7:11
- Acts 5:3
- Acts 5:5
- Acts 5:10–11

Chapter Nineteen

When the Remnant Returns

Introduction: God Watches for Return, Not Excuses

God does not stop watching when He gives people over. He stops restraining, but He continues observing. Giving over is not abandonment; it is exposure, and exposure is meant to produce clarity. Scripture never presents God as indifferent to what happens after restraint is removed. He is not waiting for explanations or emotional performances. He is watching for return.

Return is not regret. Return is not apology. Return is not sorrow alone.

Return is movement back under government.

This is why Scripture never treats restoration as automatic. Restoration is always conditional. It does not begin when people feel bad about consequences, and it does not begin when pain becomes uncomfortable. It begins when people turn back toward authority.

"If my people, which are called by my name, shall humble themselves, and pray, and seek my face, and turn from their wicked ways; then will I hear from heaven, and will forgive their sin, and will heal their land." (2 Chronicles 7:14, KJV)

The order is intentional.

313

Humbling comes before healing. Turning comes before restoration.

God does not respond to excuses. He responds to alignment.

Many experience consequences and assume suffering itself qualifies as repentance, but Scripture never teaches that. Consequence may awaken awareness, but it does not restore authority. Only return does that.

Pain does not restore government. Submission does.

This is why some suffer and never change, while others suffer and return transformed. The difference is not pain. The difference is submission. God does not restore people to independence, and He does not restore them to comfort first.

God restores people to government before He restores them to blessing.

This is where the remnant emerges. Not everyone who experiences judgment returns. Not everyone who is given over repents. Not everyone who suffers humbles themselves.

But some do.

And Scripture has a name for them.

The remnant is not defined by survival. It is defined by alignment after exposure.

This chapter is not about universal restoration. It is about who actually comes back. Because God restores those who return under authority, not those who demand relief without repentance.

Repentance Is Not Regret - It Is Return

Repentance has been weakened by being reduced to emotion. Many confuse regret with repentance and sorrow with submission. Scripture does not. Regret feels bad about consequence. Repentance changes direction back under authority.

Regret looks backward. Repentance turns around.

People can feel deep sorrow and never return. They can weep, apologize, and still refuse government. Scripture never treats tears as proof of repentance. It treats return as proof.

"Let the wicked forsake his way, and the unrighteous man his thoughts: and let him return unto the LORD, and he will have mercy upon him." (Isaiah 55:7, KJV)

Notice what is required. Ways are forsaken. Thoughts are abandoned. Direction is changed.

Repentance is not feeling bad. Repentance is moving back under rule.

This is why Scripture never says, "If they regret." It says, "If they turn." Turning requires humility. Turning requires surrender. Turning requires abandoning self-rule and returning to authority.

Many experience consequence and assume repentance has occurred because pain is present. Pain does not equal repentance. Pain may awaken awareness, but repentance requires decision.

Pain can soften pride - or harden it.

True repentance always restores alignment before it restores blessing. God does not rush comfort to people who still resist government. He restores authority first, because authority is what preserves freedom.

This is why some never recover from giving over. They want relief without return. They want restoration without submission. They want mercy without government.

Scripture does not offer that arrangement.

"He that covereth his sins shall not prosper: but whoso confesseth and forsaketh them shall have mercy." (Proverbs 28:13, KJV)

Confession alone is not enough. Forsaking is required.

Repentance that does not forsake rule does not restore authority.

Return is measurable. It shows up in obedience, not language. It appears in alignment, not explanation. When repentance is real, authority is welcomed back rather than resented.

God restores those who return. He resists those who negotiate.

Because repentance is not regret. It is return.

When Consequence Produces Clarity

Consequence does not automatically produce repentance, but it always produces revelation. When restraint is removed, reality speaks without interference. What people choose in that moment exposes whether they were restrained by conviction or merely contained by protection.

Consequence strips away illusion. It reveals what rule was desired all along.

Scripture shows this pattern repeatedly. When protection lifts, motives surface. Some harden. Some return. The difference is not the severity of consequence, but the posture of the heart toward authority.

"Before I was afflicted I went astray: but now have I kept thy word." (Psalm 119:67, KJV)

Affliction did not save the psalmist. Alignment did.

Consequence created clarity. It revealed that wandering had occurred, and clarity produced return. But Scripture also records many who experienced consequence and became more resistant, not more obedient.

Consequence reveals; it does not decide.

This is why suffering alone is never proof of repentance. Pain may interrupt behavior temporarily, but it does not change government unless submission follows. Without submission, consequence only hardens preference.

"They refused to hearken, and pulled away the shoulder, and stopped their ears, that they should not hear." (Zechariah 7:11, KJV)

Some feel pain and turn inward. Others feel pain and turn upward.

Those who return begin to see what they could not see before. They recognize how protection had been mistaken for approval and how patience had been mistaken for permission. Consequence clarifies what truth had already declared.

Clarity without return is wasted exposure.

When consequence produces repentance, obedience becomes urgent. Delay no longer feels safe. Negotiation no longer feels wise. Authority becomes desirable again, not restrictive.

God allows consequence to speak so truth becomes unavoidable. He lets reality finish the sentence correction began.

But consequence only restores those willing to return under rule.

Others learn nothing.

Because consequence does not soften everyone. It separates the remnant from the resistant.

Not Everyone Who Suffers Returns

Suffering does not guarantee repentance. Exposure does not guarantee humility. Consequence does not automatically produce alignment. Scripture never teaches that pain itself restores anyone. Pain reveals, but return is chosen.

Many endure loss and grow bitter. Many experience consequence and grow defensive. Many suffer and harden rather than humble.

Suffering removes excuses, but it does not remove pride.

"They cried unto the LORD in their trouble, and he delivered them out of their distresses. But they soon forgat his works; they waited not for his counsel." (Psalm 107:13, 43, KJV)

Scripture records deliverance followed by forgetfulness. Relief came, but alignment did not remain. This is why suffering alone cannot be trusted as evidence of repentance. Pain can break resistance - or it can entrench it.

Consequence does not change everyone. It separates those who will return from those who will resist.

Some interpret consequence as injustice rather than correction. They blame circumstances, leaders, systems, or God Himself. Their suffering produces entitlement instead of humility. Rather than returning under authority, they demand restoration on their own terms.

Scripture warns of this posture:

"Wherefore doth a living man complain, a man for the punishment of his sins?" (Lamentations 3:39, KJV)

Complaining reveals refusal. Submission reveals repentance.

Those who return stop arguing with consequence. They stop defending themselves. They stop explaining away responsibility. They accept exposure as mercy and correction as protection.

Others do not.

They endure pain but refuse government. They experience loss but resist alignment. They survive consequence without surrender.

Survival is not restoration.

This is why Scripture speaks of a remnant and not a majority. Not everyone who suffers comes back. Not everyone who is given over repents. Only those willing to return under authority are restored.

God does not measure repentance by endurance. He measures it by submission.

And only submission opens the door to restoration.

The Remnant Is Recognized by Alignment

The remnant is not identified by survival, visibility, or endurance. Scripture does not define the remnant by who made it through consequence, but by who returned under authority after exposure. Alignment - not experience - marks those God restores.

Many endure loss. Few submit after it.

The remnant is recognized by what changes after giving over. They do not merely regret outcomes; they realign under government. They do not negotiate terms; they accept correction. They do not demand restoration; they welcome rule.

"Yet will I leave a remnant, that ye may have some that shall escape the sword among the nations." (Ezekiel 6:8, KJV)

Escape is mentioned - but alignment is implied. Scripture never celebrates escape without return. Those spared are not spared to remain autonomous; they are preserved to be governed.

The remnant is not spared from authority. The remnant is restored to it.

This is why the remnant often appears smaller than expected. Many want relief; few want rule. Many want mercy; few want government. The remnant is willing to be corrected publicly and governed privately.

Scripture makes this unmistakable:

"They shall loathe themselves for the evils which they have committed." (Ezekiel 6:9, KJV)

Loathing here is not despair - it is clarity. The remnant sees what rebellion cost them and refuses to return to it. Alignment becomes precious because exposure was painful.

The remnant values authority because they have lived without it.

This is why restored authority settles quickly among the remnant. They do not resist boundaries. They do not resent restraint. They recognize that rule is protection and submission is safety.

Others call this control. The remnant calls it mercy.

God does not rebuild around talent, influence, or history. He rebuilds around alignment. Those willing to live governed are entrusted again.

The remnant is not chosen by favor. It is revealed by obedience.

And only those revealed by obedience are restored.

Restoration Always Reinstates Government

Restoration in the Kingdom of God is never cosmetic. God does not restore image without restoring authority. He does not repair outcomes while leaving government unresolved. Whenever Scripture speaks of restoration, it speaks first of rule being reestablished.

Restoration that does not reinstate government is not restoration. It is relief without alignment.

This is why God does not rush people back into position, influence, or visibility. He restores order before He restores function. Authority must be settled so freedom does not collapse again under pressure.

"Then shall ye return, and discern between the righteous and the wicked, between him that serveth God and him that serveth him not." (Malachi 3:18, KJV)

Notice what returns first. Discernment returns. Distinction returns. Government returns. Restoration is not emotional comfort - it is clarity of rule.

God never restores people to the place they fell from without addressing why they fell. He restores them to obedience

322

first. Only then does responsibility follow. Where government is not welcomed, restoration stops short.

God restores alignment before He restores assignment.

This is why Scripture repeatedly shows God testing obedience after repentance. He confirms whether authority is now embraced or merely tolerated. Restoration that bypasses this process recreates the same collapse.

"Thus saith the LORD; Stand ye in the ways, and see, and ask for the old paths, where is the good way, and walk therein, and ye shall find rest for your souls." (Jeremiah 6:16, KJV)

Rest comes after walking in the right way. Not before. God restores peace by restoring path. Government stabilizes what mercy reopens.

Those who truly return do not resist this. They welcome it. They no longer ask how quickly comfort can come back. They ask how thoroughly alignment can be restored.

Restoration that resists rule is counterfeit.

True restoration always increases submission. It sharpens obedience. It deepens reverence. Where restoration produces entitlement, something has been skipped.

God does not restore people to self-rule. He restores them to His rule.

Because only His government preserves freedom.

God Receives the Returning, Not the Resistant

God does not reject those who return. He rejects resistance.

Scripture never presents God as reluctant to restore. What delays restoration is not God's unwillingness - it is human refusal to return under rule. God's arms are open, but His Throne is not negotiable.

"If we confess our sins, he is faithful and just to forgive us our sins, and to cleanse us from all unrighteousness." (1 John 1:9, KJV)

Forgiveness is promised. Cleansing is assured. But confession here is not admission alone - it is agreement with God's judgment and submission to His authority.

God does not receive those who explain. He receives those who return.

This is why Scripture consistently contrasts humility with resistance. God does not argue with the proud. He opposes them. But He receives those who come back under His hand.

"God resisteth the proud, but giveth grace unto the humble." (James 4:6, KJV)

Resistance keeps people outside restoration even while they desire relief. Humility brings people back under covering even when consequences remain. God restores relationship before He restores position. He restores authority before He restores comfort.

God does not meet people halfway. He meets them at repentance.

Those who return do not demand explanations. They do not negotiate timelines. They do not defend what was exposed. They accept correction as mercy and authority as protection.

The resistant do the opposite. They want God's hand without His rule. They want restoration without repentance. They want relief without realignment.

Scripture does not offer that path.

"Return unto me, and I will return unto you, saith the LORD of hosts." (Malachi 3:7, KJV)

Return precedes restoration. Alignment precedes blessing.

This chapter has made one truth unavoidable: God never closes the door to return, but He never removes the requirement of submission. Restoration is always available - but only to those willing to come back under government.

God restores the returning. He resists the resistant.

And that distinction determines everything that follows.

Clarification - Submission Is to God, Not to Imitations

Submission in the Kingdom is never submission to a man pretending to be God. Scripture does not authorize human beings to replace divine authority, nor does it permit leaders to manufacture tests, control consciences, or play games with people's lives in the name of discernment.

Submission is to God's rule, not to insecure leadership seeking validation.

God never authorizes shepherds to dominate sheep, manipulate loyalty, or test people to satisfy suspicion. Leaders are not assigned to invent trials God did not give, nor to reject what God has sent because it did not arrive packaged according to preference.

"Neither as being lords over God's heritage, but being ensamples to the flock." (1 Peter 5:3, KJV)

Abusive control is not authority. Spiritual games are not discernment. Testing people to prove loyalty is not submission - it is fear-driven leadership.

True submission never violates Scripture. It never contradicts the character of God. It never replaces obedience to Christ with allegiance to personalities, systems, or platforms.

"We ought to obey God rather than men." (Acts 5:29, KJV)

When leaders reject what God sends because it does not look right, sound right, or arrive the way they expect, they are not protecting the flock - they are resisting God. And when leaders demand submission that competes with obedience to Christ, that demand is illegitimate.

Submission that replaces God is rebellion.

God restores people to His government, not to human control. He brings people back under His rule, not under manipulation dressed as authority. Any leader who requires submission beyond Scripture has already stepped out from under God's authority themselves.

The Kingdom does not function by domination. It functions by alignment.

And true alignment always points upward, never inward.

Conclusion: Return Is Proven by Realignment

Return is not proven by emotion. It is proven by realignment.

That is the final dividing line.

Not who cried. Not who suffered. Not who survived. Not who has a story to tell about what happened after restraint lifted.

Who realigned?

That is what God watches.

Because return is not regret with religious language. It is not apology wrapped in sorrow. It is not pain talking louder than pride for a moment. Return is the movement of the life back under rule. It is the surrender of self-government. It is the acceptance of correction, the welcoming of authority, and the refusal to keep negotiating with what God already judged.

This is why Scripture never measures restoration by intensity of feeling. It measures restoration by the reestablishment of government. When people truly return, their alignment changes. Their posture changes. Their relationship to authority changes. They stop defending what was exposed. They stop protecting what

God confronted. They stop asking how little they can submit and still be restored.

Realignment makes return visible.

It shows up in obedience. It shows up in humility. It shows up in teachability. It shows up in the willingness to be governed again.

That is why the remnant can be recognized. The remnant is not merely those who made it through consequence. The remnant is those who came back under rule after consequence made truth unavoidable. They do not merely want relief. They want government. They do not merely want mercy. They want order. They do not merely want God to remove pain. They want Him to restore His throne in the places where self once ruled.

And that is what separates the returning from the resistant.

The resistant still negotiate. The returning surrender.

The resistant still explain. The returning agree with God.

The resistant want restoration without rule. The returning understand that rule is the restoration.

This is why God receives the returning and resists the resistant. Not because He delights in distance, but because He will not call rebellion restoration. He will not name emotional regret repentance. He will not rebuild around lives that still resist His government.

Return is proven by realignment.

Not by confession alone. Not by consequence alone. Not by desire alone. By realignment.

So this chapter ends where the issue has always been settled: God does not restore people to independence. He restores people to His rule. And where His rule is welcomed, mercy can rebuild, clarity can remain, and authority can be trusted again.

Because in the Kingdom, return is not proven by how bad you felt when exposure came.

Return is proven by whether you came back under government.

Scripture Index

- 2 Chronicles 7:14
- Psalm 81:11–12
- Romans 1:24
- Isaiah 55:7
- Proverbs 28:13
- Psalm 119:67
- Zechariah 7:11
- Matthew 6:33
- Psalm 23:3
- Ezekiel 6:8–9
- Lamentations 3:39
- Malachi 3:18
- Jeremiah 6:16
- 1 John 1:9
- James 4:6
- Malachi 3:7
- 1 Peter 5:3
- Acts 5:29

Chapter Twenty

A Kingdom That Must Be Carried

Introduction: Restoration Creates Responsibility

Restoration is never the end of the process. It is the beginning of accountability. God does not restore people so they can return to neutrality. He restores them so they can carry what others refused to steward. Restoration transfers responsibility.

Those who return under government are not restored to comfort alone. They are restored to assignment.

Scripture never separates restoration from expectation. When God heals, He also commissions. When He forgives, He also entrusts. When He restores authority, He expects it to be carried rightly.

"To whom much is given, of him shall be much required." (Luke 12:48, KJV)

Restoration increases expectation. Authority increases accountability. Freedom increases responsibility.

This is why the remnant is not merely rescued - it is entrusted. God does not rebuild people simply to stabilize them. He rebuilds them so they can uphold what collapsed in others. The Kingdom is not carried by the gifted, the loud, or the ambitious. It is carried by those who have been corrected and remained aligned.

Restoration does not lower the standard. It raises it.

Those who return under government now bear responsibility for what they were once delivered from. They are no longer permitted to live casually with truth. They are no longer allowed to treat obedience as optional. They carry clarity that others rejected.

Scripture describes this weight clearly:

"Ye are the light of the world. A city that is set on an hill cannot be hid." (Matthew 5:14, KJV)

Light carries responsibility. Visibility carries weight. Those restored are not hidden - they are watched. How they obey now testifies to whether restoration was genuine.

This chapter is not about privilege. It is about stewardship.

Because what God restores, He expects to be carried.

Restored People Carry the Weight of Truth

Truth is never given lightly. When God restores someone, He does not simply remove shame - He entrusts responsibility. Truth carries weight, and those who have been corrected are now accountable to carry it without compromise.

Restored people are no longer learning truth for survival. They are carrying truth for stewardship.

Scripture makes this distinction clear. Truth once ignored becomes truth now guarded. What others rejected, the remnant must now hold without dilution.

"And thou shalt remember all the way which the LORD thy God led thee… to humble thee, and to prove thee, to know what was in thine heart." (Deuteronomy 8:2, KJV)

Correction produced humility. Humility produced clarity. Clarity now produces responsibility.

Those who have been restored understand the cost of resisting truth. They know what compromise leads to. They have lived through the consequences of partial obedience, delayed submission, and selective hearing.

Truth learned through collapse is never handled casually.

This is why restored people cannot pretend ignorance. They cannot claim confusion where clarity has already been given. They cannot unsee what exposure revealed.

Scripture warns against returning to neutrality after revelation:

"If the light that is in thee be darkness, how great is that darkness!" (Matthew 6:23, KJV)

Light misused becomes liability. Truth mishandled becomes judgment.

Restored people are now accountable not only for what they do, but for what they tolerate. They carry discernment others lost. They see compromise earlier. They recognize patterns faster. And silence is no longer an option.

What you see clearly, you are responsible to guard.

This is why restored people often feel pressure others do not. It is not punishment. It is stewardship. God entrusts weight only to those who have proven they will not discard it casually.

Truth is not given for discussion. It is given for obedience.

Those restored are now carriers. And carriers are accountable.

Carrying the Kingdom Requires Vigilance

The Kingdom does not drift forward on intention alone. It is carried through vigilance. What God restores must be guarded, or it will be lost again through neglect. Scripture never presents the Kingdom as self-sustaining in human hands. It must be watched, protected, and honored.

Restoration does not remove vulnerability. It increases responsibility.

Those who have been restored know this firsthand. They have lived through what happens when vigilance fades. They understand that collapse does not begin with rebellion - it begins with relaxation. When alertness drops, compromise finds room.

"Be sober, be vigilant; because your adversary the devil, as a roaring lion, walketh about, seeking whom he may devour." (1 Peter 5:8, KJV)

Vigilance is not paranoia. It is awareness.

Scripture does not call the restored to fear, but it does call them to sobriety. Sobriety is clarity. It is the refusal to live casually with spiritual responsibility. Those who carry the Kingdom cannot afford spiritual negligence, because negligence invites erosion.

What is not guarded will eventually be challenged.

This is why Scripture warns repeatedly against sleep, drift, and dullness. The enemy does not need new strategies. He waits for vigilance to weaken.

"Take heed therefore unto yourselves, and to all the flock." (Acts 20:28, KJV)

Notice the order. First to yourselves. Then to others.

Those restored must guard their own alignment before they attempt to help anyone else. Authority leaks first internally before it ever fails publicly. When vigilance is lost privately, collapse eventually appears outwardly.

Vigilance preserves what restoration rebuilt. Without it, freedom erodes quietly.

Those who carry the Kingdom learn to live alert, not anxious. They remain watchful, not suspicious. They guard obedience, not image. They protect alignment, not comfort.

The Kingdom is carried by those who stay awake.

Restoration gave them clarity. Vigilance keeps it intact.

The Kingdom Is Lost Through Compromise, Not Attack

The Kingdom is rarely lost through open rebellion. It is almost always lost through tolerated compromise. Attack is obvious. Compromise is subtle. What is resisted openly often fails, but what is accepted quietly reshapes rule from within.

Restored people do not lose the Kingdom because they are overpowered. They lose it when they stop guarding small permissions.

Scripture warns that destruction does not arrive suddenly. It grows.

"Take us the foxes, the little foxes, that spoil the vines." (Song of Solomon 2:15, KJV)

Little foxes do not announce themselves. They erode fruit quietly. Compromise begins small, justified, and rationalized. It is explained as wisdom, balance, or maturity. But every tolerated compromise shifts authority slightly away from God.

What you excuse today will rule you tomorrow.

Those who have been restored must remember how collapse began before. It was not dramatic. It was gradual. Boundaries softened. Discernment dulled. What once provoked conviction began to feel familiar.

Scripture makes this progression clear:

"A little leaven leaveneth the whole lump." (Galatians 5:9, KJV)

Leaven does not announce growth. It spreads silently.

This is why vigilance must be paired with refusal. Refusal is not harshness. It is protection. Restored people cannot afford to negotiate with compromise, because they know where negotiation ends.

Compromise always demands more than it promises.

The Kingdom does not require defenders who fight everything loudly. It requires carriers who refuse quietly. Those who walk away from what weakens alignment preserve authority without spectacle.

Restored people learn to say no early. They do not wait for compromise to become obvious. They cut it off when it is still small, because they know the cost of delay.

The Kingdom is not lost in battle. It is lost in agreement.

And agreement must be guarded relentlessly.

Carriers Are Accountable for What They Allow

Carrying the Kingdom does not only make someone responsible for what they do - it makes them responsible for what they allow. Authority is not neutral. Wherever it rests, it governs the environment around it. What is tolerated under authority eventually becomes normalized.

Restored people are no longer judged only by personal obedience. They are judged by the atmosphere they permit.

Scripture establishes this principle without ambiguity:

"Thou hast tried them which say they are apostles, and are not, and hast found them liars." (Revelation 2:2, KJV)

The issue was not personal sin. It was tolerated deception.

Jesus commended discernment because discernment protects the house. When carriers stop testing what enters, what enters begins to reshape rule. Silence becomes consent. Passivity becomes permission.

What authority does not confront, it endorses.

This is why restored people cannot hide behind humility to avoid responsibility. Silence is not humility when authority has been entrusted. Avoidance is not love when truth is at stake. God does not entrust the Kingdom to people who refuse to guard it.

Scripture warns leaders and carriers alike:

"Son of man, I have made thee a watchman… therefore hear the word at my mouth, and give them warning from me." (Ezekiel 3:17, KJV)

Watchmen are not required to control outcomes. They are required to warn.

When carriers refuse to confront what God has exposed, they become complicit in its spread. Responsibility does not require domination, but it does require clarity. Truth spoken without fear preserves authority.

God never holds people accountable for what they could not see. He holds them accountable for what they refused to address.

Those restored understand this weight. They no longer excuse compromise in the name of peace. They no longer avoid tension to preserve comfort. They guard what God entrusted, even when it costs relationship, reputation, or convenience.

The Kingdom is carried by those willing to protect it. And protection always requires courage.

The Kingdom Is Carried Forward, Not Inherited Automatically

The Kingdom is never inherited by association. It is carried by responsibility. Proximity to truth does not transfer authority, and history with God does not guarantee future stewardship. Every generation must choose alignment for itself.

Restoration does not entitle anyone to permanence. Stewardship must be renewed continually.

Scripture makes this plain. What God establishes in one season can be lost in the next if vigilance fades. Authority that is assumed instead of guarded erodes quietly.

"We have heard with our ears, O God, our fathers have told us… For they got not the land in possession by their own sword." (Psalm 44:1–3, KJV)

What God did before is testimony, not security. Past victories do not carry future obedience. The Kingdom advances only where it is actively carried.

Truth remembered is not the same as truth obeyed.

This is why Scripture warns against relying on legacy. Inherited language without inherited obedience produces hollow faith. The Kingdom does not move forward through nostalgia. It moves forward through submission.

"Every man shall bear his own burden." (Galatians 6:5, KJV)

Each carrier answers for their stewardship. Each generation must guard alignment anew. God does not judge people by what they received, but by how they carried it.

Restored people understand this. They do not assume protection because of history. They do not lean on reputation. They stay governed, because they know drift begins the moment vigilance is replaced by assumption.

What is not carried intentionally will be lost eventually.

The Kingdom is carried forward by obedience, not memory. It survives because people choose submission again and again, not because it once existed strongly.

Restoration gave them responsibility. Stewardship determines whether it remains.

Conclusion: The Kingdom Is Carried by Those Who Remain Governed

The Kingdom of God does not rest on passion, gifting, or intention. It rests on government. What God restores, He expects to be carried rightly. What He entrusts, He expects to be guarded faithfully. Restoration does not excuse responsibility - it intensifies it.

Those who carry the Kingdom are not the loudest. They are the most aligned.

Scripture never presents the Kingdom as fragile, but it does present it as selective. It remains where obedience remains. It advances where authority is honored. It withdraws where government is resisted.

"Only fear the LORD, and serve him in truth with all your heart: for consider how great things he hath done for you." (1 Samuel 12:24, KJV)

Fear preserves clarity. Service preserves alignment. Truth preserves authority.

Those restored must now live with awareness. They cannot afford casual obedience. They cannot tolerate quiet compromise. They cannot treat truth as optional or alignment as flexible. The cost of restoration was too high, and the responsibility too great.

What God restores, He expects to be protected.

The Kingdom is not carried forward by momentum. It is carried forward by submission. Every day obedience renews stewardship. Every choice either strengthens authority or leaks it.

This is why the remnant remains small. Many want restoration. Few want responsibility. Many want blessing. Few want government.

But those who remain governed become carriers.

"Be thou faithful unto death, and I will give thee a crown of life." (Revelation 2:10, KJV)

Faithfulness is not intensity. It is consistency under authority.

The Kingdom does not need more ambition. It needs more obedience.

And it will always be carried by those willing to remain governed - long after restoration, long after comfort, and long after attention fades.

Because the Kingdom does not belong to those who receive it once.

It belongs to those who carry it faithfully.

Scripture Index

- Luke 12:48
- Matthew 5:14
- Deuteronomy 8:2
- Matthew 6:23
- 1 Peter 5:8
- Acts 20:28
- Song of Solomon 2:15
- Galatians 5:9
- Revelation 2:2
- Ezekiel 3:17
- Psalm 44:1–3
- Galatians 6:5
- 1 Samuel 12:24
- Revelation 2:10

Chapter Twenty-One

The Kingdom Always Confronts

Introduction: The Kingdom Does Not Coexist With Rival Rule

The Kingdom of God never arrives quietly into hostile territory. It does not blend in. It does not adapt itself to survive. It confronts whatever already rules. Where the Kingdom enters, exposure follows. Where authority advances, resistance surfaces.

The Kingdom is not aggressive by nature. But it is confrontational by existence.

Scripture never presents the Kingdom as something that can be added alongside other authorities. It replaces them. This is why Jesus did not preach improvement - He preached invasion. The Kingdom of God does not negotiate coexistence with darkness. It displaces it.

"Think not that I am come to send peace on earth: I came not to send peace, but a sword." (Matthew 10:34, KJV)

This was not a call to violence. It was a declaration of division.

Truth divides where lies were tolerated. Authority confronts where autonomy ruled. Alignment exposes where compromise hid comfortably. The Kingdom does not create conflict - it reveals it.

Those who carry the Kingdom must understand this. Resistance is not failure. Pushback is not a sign of error. Conflict often confirms that authority has arrived.

Where there is no resistance, the Kingdom has not advanced.

This is why restored people are often shocked by opposition. They assume obedience will be welcomed. Scripture never promises that. It promises the opposite. Light exposes darkness, and darkness resists exposure.

"And this is the condemnation, that light is come into the world, and men loved darkness rather than light." (John 3:19, KJV)

The Kingdom confronts what people love when it is not God. That confrontation is unavoidable. The issue is not whether resistance comes, but whether the carrier retreats when it does.

This chapter is not about hostility. It is about steadfastness.

Because the Kingdom does not retreat to avoid conflict. And carriers are not permitted to soften truth to preserve peace.

The Kingdom always confronts. And those who carry it must decide whether they will stand.

Resistance Does Not Mean the Kingdom Is Wrong

Resistance is not evidence of error. It is often confirmation that authority has arrived. Scripture never presents opposition as a sign that truth should be adjusted. It presents opposition as the expected response when rival rule is challenged.

Truth does not provoke resistance because it is harsh. It provokes resistance because it threatens control.

From the beginning, the Kingdom has always been opposed - not because it lacked love, but because it dismantled false authority. When Jesus spoke with clarity, crowds did not become unified; they became divided. Some followed. Others withdrew. Some submitted. Others plotted.

"From that time many of his disciples went back, and walked no more with him." (John 6:66, KJV)

They did not leave because truth was unclear. They left because it was unmistakable.

This pattern has never changed. When the Kingdom advances, neutrality disappears. People must choose alignment or resistance. Silence becomes decision. Delay becomes defiance.

The Kingdom exposes allegiance.

This is why Scripture warns against chasing approval. Approval often requires dilution. Acceptance often demands silence. But the Kingdom does not expand by being accepted - it expands by being obeyed.

"Woe unto you, when all men shall speak well of you!" (Luke 6:26, KJV)

Universal approval is not a sign of success. It is often a sign of compromise.

Those who carry the Kingdom must learn this early. Resistance does not require retreat. Opposition does not require apology. The carrier's responsibility is not to be liked - it is to remain aligned.

Scripture reinforces this clarity:

"We ought to obey God rather than men." (Acts 5:29, KJV)

Obedience to God will always place carriers at odds with those who benefit from alternative rule. The Kingdom confronts comfort, exposes false peace, and challenges structures built on compromise.

Resistance does not mean the Kingdom is wrong. It means something else is being displaced.

Those who retreat at resistance reveal where allegiance truly rests. Those who stand confirm that the Kingdom - not acceptance - governs them.

Because the Kingdom does not need agreement to advance. It needs obedience.

The Kingdom Exposes What Was Hidden

The Kingdom does not create darkness. It reveals it. When authority enters a space, what has been concealed surfaces. What was tolerated becomes visible. What was excused is exposed. This is not aggression - it is illumination.

Exposure is not cruelty. It is clarity.

Scripture never treats exposure as optional. Light reveals by nature. It does not decide what to show; it simply shows what is there.

"For every one that doeth evil hateth the light, neither cometh to the light, lest his deeds should be reproved." (John 3:20, KJV)

The issue is not that the light condemns. The issue is that it reveals.

This is why the Kingdom unsettles environments built on secrecy, compromise, or unchallenged patterns. What remained hidden under tolerance cannot survive under truth. Exposure forces a decision - return or resist.

The Kingdom forces honesty.

Those who carry the Kingdom must understand this weight. When they speak truth, old alignments are disrupted. Relationships shift. Structures tremble. Resistance intensifies - not because harm was done, but because concealment was removed.

Scripture makes this unavoidable:

"Have no fellowship with the unfruitful works of darkness, but rather reprove them." (Ephesians 5:11, KJV)

Reproof is not domination. It is separation from darkness.

The Kingdom exposes not to shame, but to end rule. What is brought into the light loses its power to govern silently. Exposure removes authority from secrecy.

What is hidden rules quietly. What is exposed must answer.

Some respond to exposure with humility. Others respond with hostility. The response reveals allegiance. Light does not choose reactions - it reveals them.

Those who retreat from exposure to preserve peace forfeit authority. Those who stand allow the Kingdom to finish its work.

Because the Kingdom always exposes what was hidden. And carriers must decide whether they will remain steady when it does.

The Kingdom Divides Before It Unites

The Kingdom of God does not produce unity by compromise. It produces unity by alignment. Before it unites what can be joined, it separates what cannot coexist. Scripture never promises peace without division first. It promises truth - and truth divides.

Unity without truth is agreement. Unity with truth is alignment.

This is why Jesus did not measure success by how many stayed. He measured it by who aligned. The Kingdom does not gather crowds by smoothing edges. It gathers the faithful by drawing lines.

"Suppose ye that I am come to give peace on earth? I tell you, Nay; but rather division." (Luke 12:51, KJV)

This division is not hostility. It is exposure of allegiance.

When truth is spoken clearly, people separate themselves. Some move closer. Others move away. The Kingdom does not push them - it reveals where they already stand. Neutrality collapses when authority is declared.

Division is not failure. It is discernment.

Scripture shows this pattern repeatedly. Wherever the Kingdom advances, lines appear. Households divide. Systems fracture. Relationships strain. Not because love is absent, but because rule is being clarified.

"For the word of God is quick, and powerful… and is a discerner of the thoughts and intents of the heart." (Hebrews 4:12, KJV)

The Word divides soul from spirit, motive from action, loyalty from language. It separates what can be aligned from what must be confronted.

Those who carry the Kingdom must accept this cost. Seeking unity at the expense of truth produces false peace. Refusing division where God is dividing results in confusion and compromise.

God unites what submits. He divides what resists.

This is why the remnant often feels smaller after the Kingdom advances. Not because it failed - but because clarity arrived. Those unwilling to submit drift away when truth is no longer negotiable.

The Kingdom does not divide to destroy. It divides to reveal.

And what is revealed determines what can be joined.

Carriers Must Not Soften the Message to Reduce Resistance

When resistance rises, the temptation is always the same: soften the message to preserve peace. Scripture never authorizes this response. The Kingdom does not advance by being adjusted to avoid offense. It advances by being declared without dilution.

Softening truth does not remove resistance. It only removes authority.

Those who carry the Kingdom must understand that pressure reveals allegiance - not error. Resistance is not a signal to revise the message. It is a signal that truth has touched something ruling beneath the surface.

"For if I yet pleased men, I should not be the servant of Christ." (Galatians 1:10, KJV)

The pursuit of approval is incompatible with obedience. The moment carriers begin measuring success by acceptance, they begin trimming truth to survive. Scripture never celebrates this strategy. It exposes it.

"They have healed also the hurt of the daughter of my people slightly, saying, Peace, peace; when there is no peace." (Jeremiah 6:14, KJV)

False peace is created by softened truth. It calms resistance temporarily but leaves rule unchanged. When truth is diluted, darkness remains seated, only quieter.

Peace that requires silence is not peace.

Those entrusted with the Kingdom must resist the urge to manage reactions. Reactions belong to the hearer. Responsibility belongs to the carrier. Scripture never instructs carriers to control outcomes - only to remain faithful.

"Cry aloud, spare not, lift up thy voice like a trumpet." (Isaiah 58:1, KJV)

Clarity, not comfort, is the mandate.

Carriers who soften truth to avoid resistance may gain temporary acceptance, but they lose authority. The Kingdom does not advance through negotiation. It advances through obedience.

The message does not change because resistance increases. The carrier must decide whether obedience will remain.

Those who remain aligned allow the Kingdom to do what it was sent to do - confront, divide, expose, and restore. Those who soften truth interrupt that process and become obstacles rather than carriers.

The Kingdom does not need protection from offense. It needs faithful declaration.

And those who carry it must choose whether they will remain governed when resistance pressures them to retreat.

Standing Firm Is Part of Carrying the Kingdom

Carrying the Kingdom requires endurance, not adjustment. Scripture never promises that resistance will fade quickly. It promises that standing firm will be required consistently. The Kingdom advances through perseverance under pressure, not retreat for relief.

Standing is not stubbornness. It is loyalty under strain.

Those who carry the Kingdom must understand that opposition tests allegiance. Pressure reveals whether obedience is conditional or absolute. When resistance intensifies, the carrier's calling is not to explain truth better, but to remain aligned with it.

"Watch ye, stand fast in the faith, quit you like men, be strong." (1 Corinthians 16:13, KJV)

Standing is commanded because retreat is tempting. Scripture assumes pressure will come and prepares carriers for it. Strength here is not aggression - it is steadiness. The Kingdom is carried forward by those who refuse to be moved.

"Be not weary in well doing: for in due season we shall reap, if we faint not." (Galatians 6:9, KJV)

Weariness does not come from obedience alone. It comes from obedience under resistance.

This is why Scripture ties reward to endurance. Not everyone who starts carrying the Kingdom finishes well. Some retreat when resistance costs too much. Others stand, not because it is easy, but because alignment matters more than relief.

Standing firm is obedience extended over time.

Those who remain governed do not measure success by immediate response. They measure it by faithfulness. They do not abandon truth because it produces tension. They recognize that tension confirms authority has arrived.

Scripture gives this assurance:

"If we suffer, we shall also reign with him: if we deny him, he also will deny us." (2 Timothy 2:12, KJV)

Reigning is tied to endurance. Authority follows faithfulness. Those who stand through resistance are entrusted with greater stewardship because they have proven allegiance under pressure.

The Kingdom does not advance through force. It advances through faithfulness.

And faithfulness requires standing - again and again - until truth finishes its work.

Conclusion: The Kingdom Advances Through Faithful Confrontation

The Kingdom of God does not advance by avoidance. It advances by faithful confrontation. Wherever it is carried, it confronts rival rule, exposes hidden allegiance, divides what cannot remain joined, and demands decision. This is not cruelty. It is clarity.

The Kingdom does not seek conflict, but it never retreats from truth.

Those who carry the Kingdom must settle this reality early. Resistance is not a sign to soften obedience. Opposition is not proof of error. Pushback does not mean the message failed. Often, it means the message reached its target.

"For we wrestle not against flesh and blood, but against principalities, against powers." (Ephesians 6:12, KJV)

The confrontation is never personal, even when it feels personal. The Kingdom confronts authority, not people. When truth is declared, false rule reacts. That reaction reveals what was governing beneath the surface.

The Kingdom does not adjust to survive. It confronts to liberate.

Those who retreat to preserve peace surrender authority. Those who remain governed preserve the Kingdom. Faithful carriers do not dilute truth to remain accepted. They remain aligned and let truth do what it was sent to do.

Scripture does not promise ease. It promises victory through endurance.

"Be thou faithful unto death, and I will give thee a crown of life." (Revelation 2:10, KJV)

Faithfulness is not measured by comfort. It is measured by consistency under pressure.

The Kingdom advances because some refuse to retreat. It survives because some remain governed when resistance demands compromise. It prevails because carriers choose obedience over approval.

The Kingdom always confronts. And it always advances through those who stand.

Scripture Index:

- Matthew 10:34
- John 3:19–20
- John 6:66
- Luke 6:26
- Acts 5:29
- Ephesians 5:11
- Hebrews 4:12
- Luke 12:51
- Galatians 1:10
- Jeremiah 6:14
- Isaiah 58:1
- 1 Corinthians 16:13
- Galatians 6:9
- 2 Timothy 2:12
- Ephesians 6:12
- Revelation 2:10

Chapter Twenty-Two

Until He Comes

Introduction: Faithfulness Is the Final Measure

The Kingdom does not end with confrontation. It ends with accounting.

Scripture never presents history as unresolved. It moves toward a conclusion where every steward answers for what they carried, every authority is weighed, and every allegiance is revealed. The final issue is not gifting, fruit, or impact. It is faithfulness.

Faithfulness is not intensity. It is obedience sustained over time.

From the beginning, God has measured people not by how they started, but by whether they remained governed until the end. The Kingdom is not carried in moments of zeal, but in long obedience when attention fades and pressure remains.

"Moreover it is required in stewards, that a man be found faithful." (1 Corinthians 4:2, KJV)

Required - not admired. Faithfulness is not optional.

This is why Scripture consistently points forward. Every confrontation, every restoration, every stewardship assignment moves toward a day of evaluation. God does not forget what was entrusted. He does not overlook how authority was handled. He weighs obedience with precision.

"Behold, I come quickly; and my reward is with me, to give every man according as his work shall be." (Revelation 22:12, KJV)

The reward is not for intention. It is for stewardship.

Those who carried the Kingdom faithfully did not always see immediate results. They were not always affirmed. They were often resisted. But they remained governed. They did not abandon obedience when resistance increased. They did not soften truth to survive. They carried what God entrusted until the end.

Faithfulness is the final victory.

This chapter is not about fear. It is about finish.

Because the Kingdom is carried by those who continue under its rule until He comes.

Faithfulness Is Proven in Delay

Faithfulness is not proven when obedience is rewarded quickly. It is proven when obedience must be maintained without visible reinforcement. Scripture never equates faithfulness with speed. It ties it to endurance under delay.

Delay exposes motive. Delay reveals allegiance.

Many obey enthusiastically when results are immediate. Few remain steady when obedience is costly and affirmation is absent. Delay strips obedience of emotional reward and leaves only submission. That is where faithfulness is measured.

"Though it tarry, wait for it; because it will surely come, it will not tarry." (Habakkuk 2:3, KJV)

Waiting is not passivity. Waiting is obedience without control.

God often delays visible outcome to determine whether obedience is rooted in trust or transaction. Those who obey only when they see progress reveal that obedience was conditional. Those who remain governed without feedback demonstrate loyalty to authority, not appetite for reward.

Delay separates servants from stewards.

Scripture repeatedly emphasizes this testing ground. God entrusts truth, assignment, and authority - then allows time to pass. Not because He is absent, but because faithfulness matures only where obedience is sustained.

"Blessed is that servant, whom his lord when he cometh shall find so doing." (Matthew 24:46, KJV)

Notice the emphasis. Not finished. Not celebrated. But found faithful.

Those who carry the Kingdom until the end learn to obey without applause. They remain aligned when momentum slows. They continue guarding truth when opposition persists and progress seems invisible.

Faithfulness is obedience when no one is watching.

Delay does not cancel promise. It confirms stewardship.

Those who endure delay without drifting, compromising, or disengaging demonstrate that the Kingdom governs them - not outcome, recognition, or relief.

Because the Kingdom is not carried by those who obey quickly. It is carried by those who obey consistently.

Every Steward Will Give an Account

Faithfulness is not only tested over time - it is ultimately evaluated. Scripture is unwavering on this point. What God entrusts will be reviewed. What is carried will be weighed. What is stewarded will be answered for.

Stewardship is temporary. Accounting is certain.

The Kingdom does not drift into eternity unresolved. It moves toward a moment where every servant stands before God - not to explain intention, but to answer for obedience.

"So then every one of us shall give account of himself to God." (Romans 14:12, KJV)

This accounting is personal. It is precise. It is unavoidable.

No one answers for another's obedience. No one hides behind calling, position, or hardship. Each steward is measured by what they did with what they were given - nothing more, nothing less.

Scripture reinforces this sobering clarity:

"After a long time the lord of those servants cometh, and reckoneth with them." (Matthew 25:19, KJV)

Time does not erase responsibility. Delay does not cancel evaluation.

Those who carried faithfully do not fear this moment. They anticipate it with sobriety. Not because they were perfect, but because they remained governed. They did not bury what was entrusted. They did not trade obedience for safety. They did not excuse compromise as wisdom.

Faithfulness is not flawlessness. It is loyalty maintained.

Those who shrink back from accountability often misunderstand God's nature. This accounting is not cruelty. It is justice. It honors obedience that went unseen, uncelebrated, and unrewarded in the moment.

"Behold, the Lord cometh with ten thousands of his saints, To execute judgment upon all." (Jude 1:14–15, KJV)

Judgment here is not only for rebellion. It is for stewardship.

God does not forget what was carried. He does not overlook perseverance. He does not ignore obedience that cost comfort, reputation, or opportunity.

Nothing carried faithfully is wasted.

Every steward will give an account. And that accounting will reveal who truly carried the Kingdom until the end.

Faithful and Unfaithful Are Revealed at the End

Scripture makes a clear and unavoidable distinction: not all servants finish the same way. Everyone entrusted with the Kingdom receives responsibility, but not everyone carries it faithfully. The difference is not exposure, opportunity, or difficulty. The difference is obedience sustained to the end.

Time does not blur this distinction. It sharpens it.

Jesus spoke often about this separation, not to intimidate, but to clarify reality. The end does not reward intention. It reveals stewardship.

"The lord of that servant will come in a day when he looketh not for him… and will cut him asunder." (Matthew 24:50–51, KJV)

This is not about sudden failure. It is about prolonged neglect.

Unfaithfulness rarely appears as open rebellion. It appears as gradual disengagement. Watchfulness fades. Vigilance weakens. Authority is treated casually. What once required obedience is postponed, then excused.

Unfaithfulness begins when obedience becomes optional.

Faithful servants remain alert. They do not assume time guarantees approval. They do not confuse delay with permission. They stay governed because they understand what is at stake.

Scripture makes this contrast explicit:

"Well done, thou good and faithful servant… thou hast been faithful over a few things." (Matthew 25:21, KJV)

Faithfulness is measured in small obedience sustained consistently. It is not measured by visibility, expansion, or recognition. It is measured by whether authority was honored when no one was enforcing it.

Unfaithful servants often look active. Faithful servants remain aligned.

The end reveals what daily choices concealed. It exposes whether obedience was rooted in reverence or convenience. When evaluation arrives, the distinction is no longer debated - it is declared.

The end does not create faithfulness. It reveals it.

Those who carried the Kingdom faithfully do not fear this revelation. They are not surprised by it. They have lived prepared, not anxious, knowing that obedience - quiet, costly obedience - was never unnoticed.

Because the Kingdom belongs not to those who started well, but to those who finished faithfully.

Remain Faithful Until the End

The call of the Kingdom has never been to begin well. It has always been to remain faithful. Scripture does not celebrate starters; it crowns finishers. The weight of stewardship is not carried in bursts of obedience, but in sustained submission when strength is tested and resolve is strained.

Faithfulness is not seasonal. It is lifelong.

Those who carry the Kingdom must settle this truth: obedience does not expire. There is no point at which vigilance relaxes, submission pauses, or authority becomes optional. The end does not excuse the present. It sharpens it.

"He that endureth to the end shall be saved." (Matthew 24:13, KJV)

Endurance is not endurance of hardship alone. It is endurance in obedience.

Scripture never instructs believers to coast once they have carried long enough. It calls them to remain watchful, sober, and aligned until the final moment. Drift at the end nullifies decades of faithfulness if obedience is abandoned.

Finishing matters.

This is why Scripture warns against weariness more than failure. Weariness tempts compromise. Weariness invites justification. Weariness whispers that obedience has already been proven.

"Let us not be weary in well doing." (Galatians 6:9, KJV)

Weariness does not come from sin alone. It comes from sustained obedience under pressure.

Those who remain faithful learn to draw strength from submission, not from outcome. They do not measure success by ease. They measure it by alignment. They understand that God does not require perfection - He requires perseverance.

Faithfulness is obedience that refuses to quit.

The Kingdom is not carried by those who burn brightest. It is carried by those who stay aligned longest.

Remain faithful. Remain governed. Remain obedient.

Because the end will reveal everything.

Conclusion: Faithfulness Is What Heaven Remembers

Heaven does not remember intention. It remembers faithfulness.

Scripture never records enthusiasm, visibility, or reputation as the final measure. It records obedience. It weighs alignment. It examines whether authority was honored when obedience cost something. What matters in eternity is not how loudly someone spoke, but how faithfully they obeyed.

God does not ask whether obedience was easy. He asks whether it was maintained.

Those who carried the Kingdom faithfully did not always see results. They were not always affirmed. They were often resisted, misunderstood, and opposed. But they remained governed. They did not retreat when pressure increased. They did not soften truth when resistance intensified. They did not abandon obedience when delay tested resolve.

"Well done, thou good and faithful servant." (Matthew 25:21, KJV)

Those words are not spoken to the gifted. They are spoken to the faithful.

Faithfulness is what heaven rewards because faithfulness proves allegiance. It proves that obedience was not conditional, that submission was not temporary, and that authority was not tolerated only when convenient.

The Kingdom does not belong to those who received it once. It belongs to those who carried it to the end.

This book has traced the full arc: freedom received, obedience required, judgment revealed, restoration offered, stewardship entrusted, confrontation endured, and faithfulness tested. Every chapter has led to this final truth - the Kingdom is carried by those who remain governed until He comes.

"Be thou faithful unto death, and I will give thee a crown of life." (Revelation 2:10, KJV)

Faithfulness is not intensity. It is endurance.

It is obedience when unseen. It is alignment when opposed. It is submission when weary.

The end will not reward who began strongly. It will reveal who remained faithful.

And when all is weighed, all is revealed, and all is accounted for, the only thing that will matter is this:

Did you remain governed?

Because faithfulness is what heaven remembers.

Scripture Index

- Galatians 6:9

- Revelation 2:10

Glossary of Terms

Abundant Life (Zoe vs. Bios):

The distinction between mere natural existence and the God-kind of life. *Bios* is biological life - human survival, routine, motion, and outward activity. *Zoe* is the life that proceeds from God - Spirit-governed, Throne-sourced, and sustained by alignment to His rule.

Scripture: John 10:10; Revelation 22:1–2; John 14:6

Clarification: Abundant life is not comfort, momentum, or religious activity. A person may have *bios* and still be spiritually dry, self-ruled, and empty of God. But *zoe* is heaven's life flowing from the Throne and the Lamb into a governed vessel. This is why the book ties life to government, submission, the River, and alignment: the Kingdom is not built on *bios*, but on *zoe*.

Alignment:

Order made visible through submission to God's rule; the condition in which a life or house is brought into agreement with Heaven's pattern.

Scripture: Amos 3:3; Proverbs 29:18; 1 Peter 4:17

Clarification: Alignment is not attendance, activity, or emotional atmosphere. It is obedience made visible, and it is the first proof that government is present in a house.

Anointing:

The empowerment of the Spirit to break yokes, equip, and fulfill divine assignment and service under God's order.

Scripture: Isaiah 10:27; Isaiah 9:6–7; 1 John 2:27

Clarification: Anointing is never treated as self-authenticating. Claimed anointing without tested character, stewardship, and submission to government is exposed as unstable.

Authority:

Heaven-backed permission to act under God's rule, limited by Scripture and entrusted to those who remain governed.

Scripture: Acts 5:29; Romans 13:1; 1 Peter 5:3

Clarification: Authority is not ownership, control, title, or intimidation. It is bounded by Scripture, proven by faithfulness, and re-entrusted only where trust has been restored.

Babylonian System:

A counterfeit order opposed to God's Kingdom, marked by pride, compromise, confusion, and rebellion against divine rule.

Scripture: Revelation 18:2–4; Revelation 17:4–5; Isaiah 47:10–11

Clarification: Babylon is not merely a historical reference. It is the recurring pattern of self-rule, spiritual

corruption, and institutional compromise that resists
holiness and weakens true authority.

Flesh:

The self-directed life governed by appetite, preference, and
natural impulse rather than by God's Spirit and Word.

Scripture: Romans 8:7–8; Galatians 5:17; 1 John 2:16

Clarification: Flesh is not weakness alone. It is rival rule
inside the house - personal desire speaking as though it
were government.

Glory:

The weighty manifestation of God's presence resting upon
what He has measured, ordered, and made clean.

Scripture: Exodus 40:34–35; 2 Chronicles 7:1–3; Hebrews
12:29

Clarification: Glory is not as mood, atmosphere, or
spectacle, but as weight. Glory blesses, but it also
measures, tests, and exposes whether the house can
carry what God gives.

Government:

The active rule, order, and jurisdiction of God expressed in
a person, leader, or house.

Scripture: Isaiah 9:6–7; Romans 13:1; 1 Corinthians 14:40

Clarification: Government is not bureaucracy or rank. It
is the ruling order of the King, without which glory

cannot remain, clarity cannot endure, and the River
cannot flow rightly.

Holiness:

A life set apart from sin and consecrated for God's use;
moral and spiritual cleanliness before Him.

Scripture: 1 Peter 1:16; Hebrews 12:14; 2 Corinthians 7:1

Clarification: Holiness is not external performance or
religious image management. It is the clean condition
required for God's house to remain habitable,
trustworthy, and capable of carrying weight.

House of God:

The spiritual house God builds from people rather than
merely a physical structure; His dwelling place ordered
for His presence and rule.

Scripture: 1 Timothy 3:15; Ephesians 2:21–22; 1 Peter 2:5

Clarification: The true house is made of living people,
not stages, brands, or schedules. The question is not
whether a structure exists, but whether what is being
built can carry what God intends to place upon it.

Identity:

The self as defined by God's truth, rule, and redemptive
purpose rather than by shame, sin, or self-invention.

Scripture: John 8:32; Romans 8:15; Ephesians 4:22–24

Clarification: Identity is rebuilt when false coverings are
exposed and a person returns under truth and

authority. Identity is not self-assertion; it is restored order in the self.

Kingdom:

The reign of God confronting every rival system and bringing life under the rule of the King.

Scripture: Matthew 24:14; Luke 4:43; Romans 14:17

Clarification: Kingdom is not a slogan or church brand. It is the ruling order of God advancing into lives, leadership, and houses, displacing self-rule and confronting compromise.

Living Stones:

God's people as the material of His spiritual house, shaped and joined together for His dwelling.

Scripture: 1 Peter 2:5; Ephesians 2:19–22

Clarification: Temple language is used to show that people - not buildings - are what God is constructing. Living stones must be aligned, clean, and rightly joined if the house is to hold glory.

Mixture:

The blending of Kingdom things with compromise, uncleanness, flesh, or self-rule.

Scripture: Galatians 5:9; 2 Timothy 3:5; James 1:8

Clarification: Mixture is deadly because it weakens authority, clouds truth, makes repentance rare, and leaves the house with form but without power.

Obedience:

Active response to what God has said, expressed through surrender, submission, and faithful action.

Scripture: John 14:15; Acts 5:29; James 4:17

Clarification: Obedience is non-optional. It is the visible evidence of alignment and the practical path by which authority is carried without corruption.

Presence:

The nearness and indwelling reality of God among His people.

Scripture: Exodus 33:14; Psalm 132:13–14; Revelation 21:3

Clarification: Presence is not confused with atmosphere, crowd response, or emotional intensity. Presence belongs to what God governs, and it withdraws where disorder and compromise are protected.

Remnant:

The preserved people who remain or return under God's rule when compromise has become common.

Scripture: Isaiah 10:20–22; Romans 11:5; Revelation 12:17

Clarification: The remnant not merely as survivors, but as those who return under authority after exposure, forsaking self-rule and realigning with truth.

Repentance:

A decisive turning from sin, mixture, and self-rule back
under God's government.

Scripture: Isaiah 55:7; Proverbs 28:13; Acts 3:19

Clarification: Repentance is not regret, emotion, apology,
or consequence-awareness. It is return - direction
changed, rule welcomed back, and alignment restored.

River:

The flow of God's life and supply proceeding from His
Throne into what is governed by Him.

Scripture: Revelation 22:1–2; Ezekiel 47:1–12; John 7:38

Clarification: The River is not withheld arbitrarily. Its
flow is tied to authority, order, and the condition of the
house through which it moves.

Submission:

Yielding oneself to God's authority and the order He has
established.

Scripture: James 4:7; Hebrews 13:17; 1 Peter 5:5

Clarification: Submission is not blind compliance or
human domination. It is intelligent yielding under truth,
where obedience flows because Christ and Scripture
remain the boundary.

Throne:

The seat of divine rule from which God governs, judges,
and supplies life.

Scripture: Psalm 103:19; Hebrews 1:8; Revelation 22:1

Clarification: Throne language is used to show that every house is organized around a ruling center. Where multiple thrones exist, confusion enters; where God's Throne is honored, order and life remain.

Trust:

Proven reliability that qualifies a person or leader to be entrusted again with responsibility, authority, or stewardship.

Scripture: Luke 16:10–12; 1 Corinthians 4:2; Proverbs 25:19

Clarification: Trust is not assumed by title or charisma. It is rebuilt through hidden faithfulness, tested character, restraint, and truthful submission under God's order.

Truth:

God's standard that reveals reality, exposes darkness, and calls people into freedom and obedience.

Scripture: John 8:32; Ephesians 5:11–13; Psalm 119:160

Clarification: Truth is confrontational mercy. Truth does not negotiate with darkness; it exposes, corrects, and restores what submits to it.

Vessels:

People or ministries prepared to carry, pour, and administer what God entrusts to them.

Scripture: 2 Timothy 2:20–21; 2 Chronicles 24:14; 1
Thessalonians 4:4

Clarification: Vessels are judged by cleanness and
faithfulness, not proximity to sacred things. Clean
vessels carry life; compromised vessels leak mixture and
cannot be trusted with weight.

Weight Definition:

The substantial reality of glory and authority that tests
whether a structure, leader, or house can truly carry
what God gives.

Scripture: Exodus 40:34–35; 2 Chronicles 5:13–14;
Hebrews 12:29

Clarification: Weight is a diagnostic term. Weight
exposes foundations, reveals whether a house is
aligned, and makes clear whether what appears spiritual
is actually able to bear glory.

Scripture Index

Other Good Books
from EKI Publishing

www.ekibooks.com

- ***The Unique Factor***
  - By David Webb

- ***Escape the Shame of Babylon***
  - By David Webb

- ***Building the Kingdom Through the Local Church***
  - By David Webb

- ***Building the Temple to Hold the Glory***
  - By David Webb

- ***Unchained: Freed to be His Treasure***
  - By Kirkland M. Rite

- ***Baptized: Why did I get Wet***
  - By Kirland M. Rite

- ***Sozo: What Am I Saved From?***
  - By Kirland M. Rite

Coming from Eternal Kingdom International Publishing

Coming 2026

Soul Made Whole
By David S. Webb

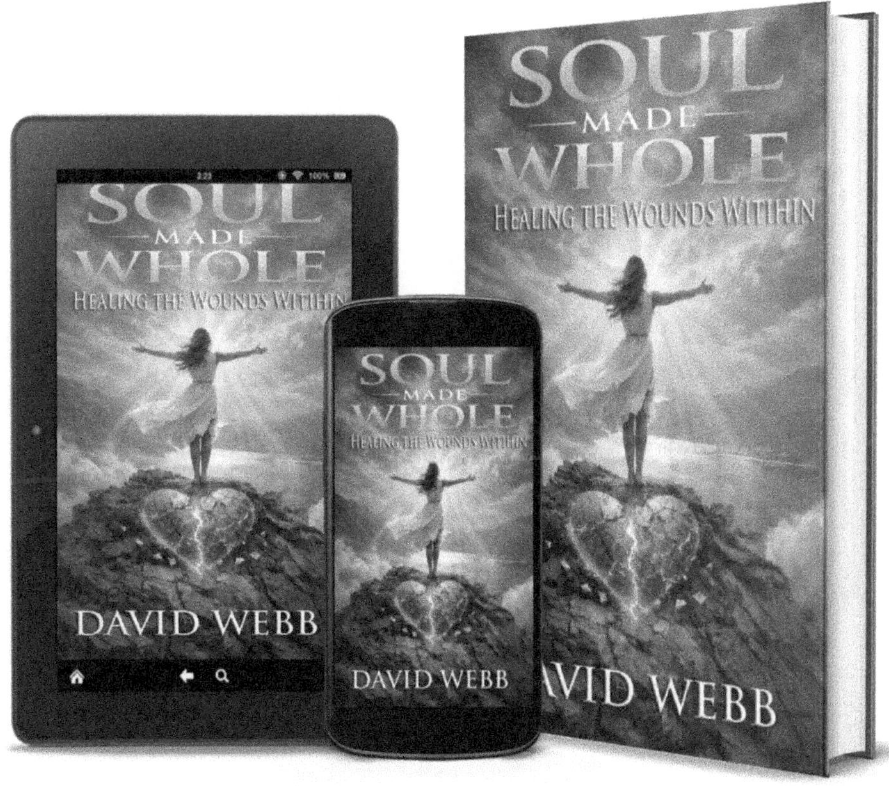